The Not-So-Scary Guide to Ghosts

THE NOT-SO-SCARY GUIDE TO GHOSTS

How to Make the Paranormal *Normal*

Rebekah "The Ghost Guide" Carmichael

ADAMS MEDIA

NEW YORK AMSTERDAM/ANTWERP LONDON TORONTO SYDNEY/MELBOURNE NEW DELHI

Adams Media
An Imprint of Simon & Schuster, LLC
100 Technology Center Drive
Stoughton, MA 02072

First Adams Media hardcover edition July 2026

ADAMS MEDIA and colophon are registered trademarks of Simon & Schuster, LLC.

Interior design by Kellie Emery
Interior images © Adobe Stock; Getty Images

Manufactured in China

10 9 8 7 6 5 4 3 2 1

Library of Congress Cataloging-in-Publication Data has been applied for.

ISBN 978-1-5072-2637-7
ISBN 978-1-5072-2638-4 (ebook)

DEDICATION

To the younger version of me, who needed this book. To the countless others who learned along with me through socials, consults, and community. To my mom, who loved me through all the weird. To Tharyn, whose belief in me never faltered. To Hermes, who played psychopomp to my spiritual journey. To Rupert, who taught me fate was real. To the ghosts who challenge me to continue growing. Thank you.

TABLE OF CONTENTS

PREFACE

The first rental house I toured in Wilmington, North Carolina, was originally built in 1910. The wood floors creaked. The foundation tilted slightly sideways. At over one hundred years old, the windows did little to insulate the awkwardly shaped rooms. As the real estate agent and my roommate began to discuss the lease, I took to wandering through the rooms on my own.

Despite knowing I was alone, I couldn't shake the feeling someone was watching me. The unexplainable feeling of invisible eyes followed me as I went from room to room. When the feeling backed away as I walked closer to the main bathroom, I was suddenly convinced I had made up those perceptions.

As I entered the bathroom, my eyes were drawn to an area in the far corner of the room, in front of the closet door. My breath caught as the corner seemed to become darker despite the sun shining through the nearby window. The image of a middle-aged man popped up in my mind's eye. I felt uneasy and anxious. I blinked a few times and refocused my vision. The darkness seemed to dissipate. I pushed the image out of my mind. This made no sense. Maybe I was just tired and my eyes were doing strange things? This whole thing had to be my overactive imagination. It was all in my head—right?

What I would have done to have *The Not-So-Scary Guide to Ghosts* at that time!

I'm Rebekah The Ghost Guide, and I first reached viral TikTok status in 2019 when I was a ghost tour guide in Wilmington, North Carolina. I'd already developed a reputation with the other tour guides; they said they always knew when I was coming up to a location—not because of my physical presence, but rather due to the spikes in paranormal activity, often captured by guests' cameras, that happened when I was nearby. Having collected some of these photos from both my own tours and others', one day I decided to make and post five fifteen-minute videos asking TikTok viewers to tell me what they saw in the photos. I woke up to 15,000 followers the next day and 150,000 followers a few months later, and the rest is history.

Looking back at my life, I now realize that I'd been having spiritual experiences from a very young age, since long before that first apartment in Wilmington. As a child, I often saw shadows and unexplained transparent figures. These frightened me, but when I finally built up the courage to express my fears to my parents, I was told that I must have been dreaming, that all I had to do was say a prayer and all would be well. Well, pray I did. I prayed to my own power, to my own will, and to what I thought of as "angels," who I believed could help me. While I couldn't have known this at the time, those "angels" were spirit guides sent to work with me and help me grow my abilities.

As I grew up, I had a touch-and-go relationship with the spirit world. My spiritual perceptions increased during my early teen years. At that time, seeing figures and auras ended up, more than once, protecting me in the midst of risky and dangerous situations. As life calmed down and I found myself farther from the situations of my early teens, my abilities lessened. It wasn't until my late twenties, when I was living in Raleigh and Asheville, North Carolina, that I began to slow down enough to hear my own thoughts. On a whim, I got a dog, Mira, and it was by her encouragement that I finally began to reconnect with nature and, in turn, myself. To this day I consider Mira an incarnate spirit guide. With her help, I realized my life needed a swift pivot. I moved to Wilmington for no other reason than that I liked walking the sidewalks and looking at old houses. Little did I know that that move would unlock parts of my life that I had never even believed in before.

My mediumship reawakening started with my moving to a highly haunted house and then leading ghost tours. As a global pandemic quieted the world, I began to understand that I may have been talking to ghosts my whole life without really realizing it. It took years for me to build my ability to perceive spirits and to feel comfortable calling myself a psychic medium. The good news is it doesn't have to take *you* years to strengthen and believe in your spiritual perceptions. When I was going through this, I had no teacher. You do.

Throughout this book, I will be sharing stories of how my psychic skills have grown. Through trial and error, through meeting thousands of people, and through talking to ghosts on the street, I have grown into what I am today. Over the years, I've worked with over a thousand clients one-on-one, recorded hundreds of videos, taught monthly how-to courses and live workshops, and been invited speak at conferences and events across the country. I've been interviewed internationally on morning talk shows, been written about in national and international magazines, and appeared on an array of podcasts and livestreams.

I've been a viral Internet sensation, a ghost enthusiast, a spiritual activator, and just a person who enjoys talking to ghosts. My goal is to show you, through my own experiences, that meeting and communicating with ghosts does not have to be like the scary interactions you see conjured up on TV or in the movies. Like the living, ghosts have many types of personalities and temperaments, and if you protect your energy and approach ghosts with respect and dignity, you have very little to fear. I hope you enjoy the stories in this book and allow them to help you understand more about your abilities and about the ghosts around you.

INTRODUCTION

If you've ever felt a presence you couldn't identify, seen a shadow shift into something more material, or heard voices directing you and wondered if it was possible that you might be picking up on something supernatural—then this book is for you! Ghosts can be anywhere, and communicating with them does not have to be a scary or complicated process. In fact, because all of us have intuition, we all have the potential to connect to the other side.

In *The Not-So-Scary Guide to Ghosts*, you'll discover easy and fun instructions for finding and connecting with ghosts without feeling intimidated or frightened. Rather than getting wrapped up in the technical aspects of paranormal investigations, you will enhance your natural, intuitive gifts. I'll show you how you can communicate with ghosts on *your* terms. Together we will make the paranormal less intimidating and spooky and more, well, *normal*.

This book will help you prepare for, initiate, and explore ghostly interactions. We'll talk about:

- What ghosts are (and aren't).
- How to be aware of—and protect—your energy when getting ready to communicate with ghosts.
- How to shield yourself so spirits don't follow you home.
- Both technological and psychic tools you can use to communicate with spirits.
- The right way to start a conversation with a ghost.
- What to do with the information from your ghost reads.

Plus, in every chapter, you'll find some of my personal stories of meeting and talking to ghosts—so you can know what to do (and what not to do!) if you find yourself in similar situations. These stories will give you real-life examples of how to use the steps presented in this book.

With *The Not-So-Scary Guide to Ghosts*, you'll find the encouragement you need to start connecting with spirits. There's so much you can learn from ghosts—if you only believe in your power to talk with them!

CHAPTER 1

GHOSTS AND MEDIUMSHIP

Before you begin to hone your ghost communication skills, it's important to have a basic understanding of what ghosts are and how they perceive us (and vice versa!). Everyone seems to have a different definition of what a ghost is, but the good news is that as long as a definition doesn't harm anyone—ghosts included—there's nothing wrong with having different opinions. In this chapter you'll learn about the frequencies and densities of ghosts, as well as some common kinds of entities. I'll also be sharing what *I* believe a ghost is for your consideration. Lastly, you'll learn about psychic mediums and how they communicate with these different types of spirits.

WHAT ARE GHOSTS?

If you were to ask a group of people what they think a ghost is, chances are you'd get a variety of answers. Rather than being discouraging, these answers prove how much there still is to learn about ghosts. We all have different minds, backgrounds, religions, and cultures, so it's not surprising that the subject of ghosts often causes deep thought, varied feelings, and curiosity. As you move forward in your work with ghosts and with your own understanding of what a ghost is, remember to keep an open mind.

GHOSTLY GO-TO

Ghosts may have many kinds of associative names, depending on the culture explaining the paranormal event. *Phantom*, *wraith*, *haint*, *specter*, *presence*, *vision*, *soul*, and *spirit* are only a few.

In a world where many psychic mediums take a very black-and-white stance on whether spirits stick around or move on after death, I have found a more colorful explanation. In my experience, ghosts are the pieces of souls that are not ready to move on to the next plane of existence. This means that there can be a fuller soul of a passed loved one out there on the other side who is doing just fine, but at the same time a ghost of them may lag around guarding their favorite chair. Keep in mind that spirits are not bound by the physical. That means that they can exist in two places at once. A ghost may represent only a moment in a life, whereas the fuller soul may connect and remember much more.

The fact that ghosts are just pieces of souls means that some ghosts may not fully remember elements of their lives. They may understand that they are at home, but they may not understand that they died. You should always consider that the ghost you're speaking with may have a kind of memory loss, and you should have patience with them. The ghost may remember elements of their favorite music but may have forgotten their own name. Keep in mind that the ghost is a fragment that maintains a connection to something physical, even when that physical element may have long moved on.

This is my opinion, now, about what a ghost is, but I admit my views have changed over time. I used to believe that a soul either stuck around in a place as a ghost, with the people they loved, or they moved on to either an afterlife space or to be reincarnated. It was only through experience and research that my view widened. I admit that the concept of pieces of souls was hard to take in at the beginning! I was meeting souls who had both moved on and were still ghosts? Shouldn't that be a contradiction? Keep in mind that spirits are fluid and nonphysical. Just as, to remember a specific incident from your life, you may need to be in a specific place or be asked a certain question to jog your memory, so too can portions of a spirit remain connected to different physical places while the rest of the soul moves on.

SPIRITUAL VIBRATIONS, FREQUENCY, AND DENSITY

Vibration is the inherent energetic quality of an object, environment, or person. This force may influence how we understand, interact with, and perceive the world around us. Spiritual beings are understood to give off vibrations, just as those in the physical world naturally vibrate on a molecular level. Similar to electromagnetic vibration, much of the spectrum of spiritual vibration cannot be seen. But like vibrations in the physical world, spiritual vibrations can be felt, heard, and perceived, especially as they become more abundant. Spiritual vibrations may affect the physical world—vibrations may cause a low rumble or cause glass to crack—but it is possible to feel and understand vibrations without succumbing to them.

How a person feels around different types and qualities of spirits says more about their own physical inclination than it does about the spirit being "good" or "bad." To understand what part of a soul you may be talking to, it's important to understand some of the qualities of spirits—particularly their vibrations' frequency and their density.

Frequency

Frequency, by definition, is the number of cycles or vibrations a wave (for example, a sound wave) completes within a set amount of time. Sound frequency can be measured in hertz, and yes, spiritual vibration, too, can be measured in this way, with paranormal investigative equipment. Frequency is connected to qualities such as wavelength and wave speed. For a simple example of frequency, imagine a long rope held up by two people. If one person moves their end of the rope up and down, the whole rope moves in a wave pattern. The faster the rope is moved, the higher the frequency of the waves. This is a way of visualizing the invisible waves all around us.

Just as high- and low-frequency sound waves are neither good nor bad, neither are different types of spiritual vibrations. Therefore, when I speak of low-frequency spirits, I don't mean they are bad. When I speak of high-frequency entities, I do not mean they are good. I merely mean that there are entities close to this plane and our human understanding, and there are those that exist farther away.

Density

A material's density is the amount of mass it has per unit of volume. Density is the reason why two objects of the same shape and size may have very different weights. One with a lighter density will float in water or even in air, whereas an object with a heavier density will sink. You wouldn't think a whale was bad simply because it couldn't fly like a bird, would you? High or low density does not necessarily mean good or bad.

Spirits may work in a similar fashion. An underworld god may have a heavier density but may have a high frequency, just as an upperworld god may have a lighter density with a matched high frequency. *Under*, in this case, can merely be understood as *dense*. Ghosts often have a heavy density as well as a low frequency. Frequency is often measured with electronic equipment that records audio and seismicity, whereas density may be more commonly witnessed through visual recording. As humans, we oftentimes have a naturally heavy density compared to many other spirits—for example, passed loved ones and spirit guides. That doesn't make us bad; rather, it allows us to be grounded in this physical plane as long as we're here. Similarly, ghosts may have a very heavy density, often heavier than our own, but once again, that does not make them bad or out of place.

GHOSTLY GO-TO

Physicists have long studied unseen entities using thermal radiation, electrons, and anomalous microwave emissions. They've even been able to explore dark matter. We are at the precipice of scientifically observing sentience and emotion behind these elements!

Being in the presence of an entity with a different density or vibrational frequency can make you feel uncomfortable. However, it's important to learn to navigate the difference between uncomfortable and dangerous. These shifts can cause your physical senses to react. Sometimes, if the change is too uncomfortable, you may decide to change your environment. This can be done by simply stepping away to take a breath or by leaving a spot entirely. Always remember that you are in control of your own comfort. That said, your discomfort does not always mean danger. It's up to each individual to figure out what level of discomfort is okay for them in a given moment.

HOW TO NAVIGATE SPIRITUAL FREQUENCY AND DENSITY

The various combinations of spiritual frequency and density are like the various parts and systems of a tree. The roots are no better than the branches, and vice versa—each part serves a function for the life and balance of the tree's health. Low frequencies are like the roots. We, as physical beings, naturally sit either near the roots or just at the base of the tree where it comes out of the ground. With practice, we can sink into the roots, just as we can sit in the branches. For this metaphor, the roots are closely related to ghosts as I described them earlier—fragments of souls that aren't ready to move on to the next plane of existence. The branches of the tree represent the energy of gods. Keep in mind that ghosts may be neither all good nor all bad, and the same goes for the gods. All exist to make up the whole, balanced tree.

Some mediums are skilled at picking up and connecting with ghosts. That means that their natural frequency is set closer to our existence on the physical plane where ghosts are naturally situated. This also means that the typical person may be able to connect with ghosts or passed loved ones easier than other kinds of spirits. Imagine sitting in sand or under a weighted blanket. It may be a little bit difficult to move around to see into the sky or the leaves of the tree, but at any point you could easily wiggle yourself out to look at higher points. However, that "wiggling out" process is sometimes a skill that requires practice. Follow these steps to navigate spiritual frequencies:

1. To practice, imagine yourself sitting at the base of a tree. As you sit—either in your mind's eye or physically—think to yourself how comfy it is to be near the ground where you don't have to exert yourself. Get comfortable being there. Be observant of your own density and gravity. This is where you connect to other living souls.
2. Now, lie down and really try and feel the roots of the tree protruding from the ground. It may be a little uncomfortable to feel these roots, but it is not necessarily dangerous. Make your observations. Feel the weight of your body over the ground.
3. Next, stand up. This is a good representation of where passed loved ones and some spirit guides may sit. Notice how you can see more around you from this angle. Once again, be present and take in the differences you've experienced as you've moved from sitting to lying down to standing.
4. If you're feeling adventurous, it's time to get into the branches of this tree. Imagine what you may find in the branches. Does the air feel any thinner? Are there birds, bugs, or critters? If so, what can you learn from their existence so high up? At this level, you can also look down. How does your perspective change from this angle?

Some mediums are skilled in speaking to higher powers such as gods and collective consciousness. Think of working at this frequency as like sitting on top of the tree or even in the space above it. Keep in mind that, at that high angle, you may not be able to see the base of the tree, let alone the roots. If you've only ever connected with gods in the branches of the tree, it may be hard for you to imagine that the roots (or ghosts) exist, but it is important to keep a level head and navigate all the frequencies.

GHOSTLY GO-TO

Tibetan monks have been scientifically studied for their ability to raise their body temperature through meditative practices. They do this through breathing techniques and focusing on visualizing inner heat. Similar techniques have been used by psychic mediums for spiritual meditation and connection.

A habit that helps me connect to different spiritual frequencies is to adjust where I'm physically looking. The entities aren't literally physically below or above us; rather, changing position can help our physical bodies understand what we're talking to. While it may feel a little funny at the beginning, using different physical positions for different entities can be beneficial to your clarity in the long term. I tend to look down when connecting with a ghost. I look straight forward when talking to a passed loved one. I look slightly upward when I'm talking to a spirit guide, and I look way up or close my eyes and sit up straight when I'm talking to a god.

Whether it's utilizing the image of a tree or looking up or down to where spiritual vibrations with a certain frequency may be, you may consider that the higher you perceive a being's frequency to be, and/or the lower their density, the higher in this metaphorical tree they are. Conversely, the lower their frequency and/or the higher their density, the closer to the roots the being is.

DIFFERENT KINDS OF "ENTITIES"

Not all spirits and spiritual activity are the same. While one particular energy may be able to affect another form of energy, there are also some energies that can exist independent of each other. The reason for understanding frequency and density is to be able to better classify the spiritual energy you may encounter. In addition to these aspects, you also need to understand the different energetic beings that exist all around you.

Non-Sentient Energy

Have you ever walked into a place and felt different without any indication as to why the energy changed? Perhaps you walked into a new room and suddenly felt dread, only to discover later that there'd been a tragic death there. Or maybe it was the opposite: You crossed the threshold of a holy site and suddenly felt lighter. In either of these cases, you may have actually walked into a thought-form spirit.

Thought-form spirits are created by the energy of cognition; however, they may not have sentience. For example, sometimes when people step onto battlefields, they get visions of people and things long gone, or hear sounds of guns that haven't fired in a hundred years, or feel faint phantom pain, as if they've been wounded. These may all be caused by non-sentient thought-form spirits. This is energy that can be felt but not necessarily communicated with.

Fascinatingly enough, these spirits have been recorded through paranormal investigative technology. I've heard music playing decades after the musicians left. However, if I ask the music to come back, it rarely does anything different. If anything, I may hear the same few notes of a song repeated, and that's it. Such energy may repeat as if it were on its own record; when the source is non-sentient energy, it's unlikely the song can be changed for the listener. This is also why you may hear cries of "Charge!" at a battlefield while never being able to find the ghost who uttered them. Until the energy moves, the sound will repeat. It doesn't necessarily mean there's someone to talk to, but it makes for great evidence and validation!

Inhuman Entities

Inhuman entities are not necessarily scary. Inhuman entities are often hybrids of various beings and can sometimes sit at different frequencies. I once met an entity that was a cross between deer legs, a tree-branch top, and the soul of a man who said he lived 6,000 years ago. I wouldn't have believed what I was picking up on at the time if a local shaman had not told me he heard and saw the same being.

Other beings may be anything from fae to aliens to mythological beasts. Sometimes they collect around a particular area, and lore may build about them. Other times they come and go for their own reasons. Many entities exist. They're serving their own purposes, and every so often an entity's path crosses ours, like a kind of Venn diagram of intersecting energy. Your picking up on their presence doesn't mean there's something you can or should do about it. Sometimes, they're just there.

Naturally, inhuman entities may make us uncomfortable. Some of them make us think we're looking at living nightmares, but that is not the case. They are just no longer human (or they never were). This means that they may not even show up on your devices or tech. They may not share your rules or morals. Some may not even belong in your path; they're simply trying to do what they need to do to move on. It's best to treat each one as an individual and act according to what you feel is best to do.

Ghosts

As previously mentioned, a ghost is a fragment of a fuller soul that has since moved on. Some ghosts remember many elements of their life and can be fascinating conversationalists; others may be stuck on a singular object or place or interest, and sadly some are stuck in a loop of fear surrounding a traumatic event of their life. It's important to remember that ghosts are individuals. They can be found in different stages of sentience and ability. Energy is neither created nor destroyed—it's always somewhere. If a ghost is not causing a problem to themself or others, please leave them be. Ghosts do not exist for us to play savior and move them on. They can simply be. Some ghosts may be interested in conversation and connection, but some are not. It's important to treat each spirit as an individual, to listen to them, and to offer them what dignity you can while still maintaining your own boundaries and self-respect.

Passed Loved Ones

Passed loved one is a catch-all term for anyone who has lived an incarnation and has since transitioned from our physical plane to the next. When I say *passed loved one*, I'm talking about the fuller part of the once-incarnate soul—the part that does not get stuck behind. If you hear a medium saying that your passed loved one has left no ghosts and that everything is remembered and without pain on the other side, it is because the loved one's natural level of frequency never gets lower than the trunk of our frequency tree.

In my experiences, passed loved ones often have a time of growth and reflection once they get to the other side. This process may take just a little time or longer, depending on what they need. I find that those who have made peace with their lives are the ones mostly likely to graduate from their reflection time sooner. However, if they're trapped in guilt, shame, and insecurity, their reflection time can take much longer. I often recommend that people allow time for passed loved ones to explore this reflective process. Sometimes they may be around at a lower frequency for a few weeks to even some months as they want to be close to loved ones during this transitional process that they are undertaking. It's a natural and important part of their personal progress to eventually take the necessary time for themselves to process their life on their own terms.

It may be difficult to reach out to them during this time, as they have to have some sense of removal from us in order to best understand the lessons they need to learn. If there are a lot of lessons to review, they may feel farther away for longer. It's important to keep in mind that a passed loved one's distance may have less to do with their wanting to be so far away, and more to do with them taking the time to better understand themselves before making any further connections with us. However, I still encourage people to reach out as they like! This process will feel similar to sending a card through standard "snail" mail. You may not always know when the word is received. You may not always know when you'll get a reply. You just have to trust that a response will come back to you when the time is right. Reach out to your passed loved ones without preset expectations. Most importantly, be sure that you're doing whatever mindfulness and mental health practices you need to do to grieve the changes that come with physical loss. Spiritualism is not a substitution for mental health practice.

GHOSTLY GO-TO

This reflection time is the reason why I am such an advocate of mental health while you're alive. There is a direct correlation between your now and your after.

Pets can also be passed loved ones! The best news is, they oftentimes require little to no reflection and transition time, regardless of how they passed. Cats are especially talented at deciding when they're ready to make themselves known in the afterlife. However, in my personal experience, I've seen dogs pop right into spirit immediately after passing as well. There is certainly something to be said about living a simple life of love and ease.

Spirit Guides

What are spirit guides? They are the entities who work specifically with you to help you on your life path. Spirit guides take many different forms:

- Sometimes they are your ancestors.
- Sometimes they knew you from past lives or incarnations.
- Some may be your passed loved ones (even pets!).
- Others may be inhuman entities such as fae, elementals, and aliens.

Can ghosts be spirit guides? Not exactly. A true spirit guide can put their own personal needs and biases aside to assist an incarnate person with what they need to achieve for themselves. Ghosts, while they may be able to offer spiritual guidance, cannot be formal guides as they, at their frequency, are likely still connected to their own needs. Similarly, passed loved ones may not always be true guides if they are too connected to their needs over your own. For example, if Grandma is pushing you to go to church but you know church isn't for you, that's *her* need for you, not *your* need for you.

Some spirit guides may follow you from birth to death, whereas others may pop in to assist with one specific aspect of your life and pop out. Their frequency often sits where the trunk of the tree meets the branches, but it may be in the branches as well. In some cases, people may share spirit guides. Think of them as collaborators on your journey. It is up to you to decide what you're going to do. Spirit guides assist you in making the most educated decision with the information at hand—they do not do the work for you.

Deities

Deities are the branches of the frequency tree. They possess the ability to look down at the other frequencies as well as look up into the collective consciousness of energy and thought. There are many different kinds of deities, and their lore stretches back to the very beginning of societal connection. Humans have always sought to understand the world around them and why things were the way they were. Deities assisted in that understanding.

Some deities came about from a need. For example, there are many deities of harvest and fertility. Did the deity first exist, only to be learned of and worshipped? Or was the deity created based on the requirements of civilization? Depending on which culture and mythology you're looking at, the origin story may change.

Deities, as they are so far away in frequency from ghosts, often have little to do with them—the exception being those who work as reapers and psychopomps (movers of spirits). As these deities are often skilled at adjusting their frequency, those who regularly work in lower frequencies may have an easier time picking up on them.

GHOST STORY

GRANDAD OR GHOST?

I used to think that all energy stayed at the same frequency. For example, I used to believe that if someone was staying on this physical plane as a spirit, they must either be trapped in a location as a ghost or be able to move around and follow friends and family as a passed loved one. As I began to expand my ability to understand spiritual frequencies, I realized that there could be many more layers to consider and that it was important for me to be able to mark the differences between them to get a more accurate psychic mediumship connection. This story is an example of that concept.

In one of my most complex psychic mediumship consultations to date, a client booked with me due to a mysterious paranormal event that had started to occur in her family home. The client told me that almost every night she and other members of her household would hear heavy boots going up the stairs to the second floor. She said she had lived at the house for a while, but this occurrence was relatively new, and it was beginning to scare her kids.

I looked into the energy and found the culprit. I described to her a man in his forties. He was wearing work clothes and big heavy boots, and he smelled of machinery. His en-

ergy felt very drained, as if he were carrying much weight on his shoulders. As I began to describe the man's facial features, the client's face dropped in astonishment.

"That's what my grandfather looked like in his forties," she told me, "He worked at a factory."

She told me that she had inherited his house but had never picked up on him in this way before. She said she'd thought she felt him on and off over the years and was confused why he would show up in such a loud way now. To her, his energy had always felt at peace, so she was confused about why he felt so burdened. The other oddity was that he had passed well into his eighties. Why was he showing up in his forties and suddenly acting like a ghost?

Through some energetic investigation, I decided to look at the situation from a different point of view. I asked the client if I could connect with her energy and then connect through her with the passed loved one, her grandfather. I needed to see if he had somehow fallen from where he'd been or if there was something else going on. Once I found the part of her grandfather that was more closely connected to her, I realized the problem.

I asked the grandfather about the time in his life when he was in his forties. He explained that it was a very complicated time. He felt as if he was unable to support his household as he needed to, and it was very burdensome. He worked late nights and was always very tired when he got home. I asked him if he thought it was possible he had left a remnant of himself behind in that time so that he could move forward in life. When he agreed it was possible, I asked if he was willing to accept that part of him so that it wouldn't haunt his house anymore. He said he was ready, and I helped to facilitate the transition of energy.

When I followed up with the client some months later, she told me that after we had worked together, the loud events on the stairs had immediately stopped. She said the house felt better, and even though she never told her young kids what happened, they were no longer afraid of the stairs. It was a true night-and-day difference. We then thought through events surrounding the haunting and concluded that it had likely occurred because of two factors. First, the woman's family members were having a stressful time at work, and that stress was getting harder to leave at the front door. Second, they had recently moved some old family heirlooms around in the basement and attic—items that had belonged to her grandfather.

This experience was incredibly eye-opening to me. It detailed that both a ghost and a passed loved one could exist in different places at one juncture. The passed loved one could be in an afterlife space and still have left a piece behind to process here on the physical plane. As the healing journey is far from a linear one, this spirit's journey revealed to me that healing can continue to happen in all areas of life, even after death. I learned that everyone has an opportunity to heal at the time that is meant for them, and I continue to be inspired by this story to this day.

GHOSTS AND MOBILITY

Ghosts may have the ability to move around. They also may have the ability to pop out of one location and into another (without traveling through the space in between), as they don't have physical bodies that must move through space and time. I've heard of famous ghosts haunting numerous places. For example, President Thomas Jefferson is said to haunt Monticello, his home near Charlottesville, Virginia, but I've also heard he's seen with his collection of books, which is kept at the Library of Congress in Washington, DC.

On the other hand, some ghosts can get stuck in immobility. I once saw the ghost of a man stuck at a table in the middle of a Waffle House in downtown Wilmington, North Carolina. It was like he had been walking, slowed down too much, and then never moved again. One ghost from my previous haunted home was always looking out of the closet of the main bathroom. He never moved, and at the time I didn't know what to do to help him. As for the man at Waffle House, with the help of some friends I have who are in spirit, I was able to awaken him enough so he could move to another location and wouldn't stay stuck at a table. Sometimes ghosts get stuck because part of their energy gets tethered to a space or thing that they're either consciously or unconsciously unwilling to make peace with and let go. Sometimes ghosts lose momentum. It's similar to how a person may be unwilling to rise from their desk during the day, or so unwilling to get up from the couch at night that they find themselves sleeping there. This is why it's important for us all to keep moving around and encourage our energetic spaces to do the same.

Momentum creates momentum; that's as true for energetic movement as it is for physical movement.

GHOSTLY GO-TO

If a ghost is not harming anyone and peace can be found through compromise in a space, I may work with the ghost to encourage memory and momentum, but I will otherwise leave them alone to figure out whatever it is they need to figure out to exist where they are.

The mobility of a ghost is tied to its frequency. Ghosts are not stagnant; they can stretch their abilities. So, over time, they may raise their frequency on their own and be able to travel more freely. Sometimes they may need a little help from someone who can mutually and consensually connect with them to move them around. For example, I've worked with ghosts who I'm friends with to help them be able to speak to me regardless of how far away I am from them. I've also worked with ghosts to enable them to travel with me so that they can see new sights, and I've helped them to get back to their comfortable haunts afterward. I've also worked with them to stay where they are with greater comfort to their energetic space.

HOW GHOSTS AND MEDIUMS PERCEIVE EACH OTHER

It is often said that some ghosts perceive psychic mediums as having a sort of glow around them. There are a couple of different versions of this claim:

- The activation of psychic senses produces a glow that can be picked up on by those looking for guidance.
- The colors of a medium's aura draw a ghost in.

This glow may show up around a person's heart or head, or around their form in general. Other times, similarly to how we in the physical realm may be drawn to other people without clearly understanding why, ghosts may simply be drawn to those who they think may be able to see them and speak with them. While the psychic medium "glow" is not an exact science and may be debated, the general understanding that there can be a glow has been widely validated as something spirits (and other psychics) may perceive.

GHOSTLY GO-TO

Some ghosts may see you exactly as you present yourself physically. Occasionally, a ghost may see you and be reminded of someone they knew in life. They may see you as interchangeable with the person they knew, especially if they don't have a strong understanding of how much time has passed since they died.

Mediums' perceptions of ghosts may differ from person to person, depending on what psychic skills they have. I've heard of some clairvoyants seeing ghosts as clearly and vividly as they see other living people. However, this isn't always a consistent skill; seeing one ghost very vividly does not automatically mean that the next ghost will be as clear. Most often, people see a ghost for a moment in passing. Until proven otherwise, the brain registers the experience as something that happened in the physical world. Due to a variety of factors, including level of psychic perception, mindset, and sometimes even the time of day, how a ghost looks to a living person at a passing glance will vary. Generally speaking, ghosts are seen as transparent, and often some features can be very vivid while others are not.

In general, whenever I'm asked whether ghosts can see us or vice versa, I present the counter question, "How often do you see other people?" We live in a loud and busy world where we may often miss a person standing on the other side of the street or even someone sitting next to us on a bus. We pull our focus into whatever we're doing, and we may miss details about others all around us. Ghosts may be the same. If they're searching for someone who can see them, they may find them. However, if that person is not paying attention, the connection may be missed. If you're worried this has happened to you, please allow yourself some grace. How often have you missed a text from a friend? How often, when someone has called out to you, have you not heard them in time before moving on? Trust that if the interaction, physical or spiritual, is meant to happen, it will.

WHAT IS A PSYCHIC MEDIUM?

Nowadays, the term *psychic medium* has become a prominent term in the field, but what is a psychic medium, and how are today's mediums different from the mediums of the past? Let's break down the terms *psychic* and *medium* individually before we combine them.

Psychic is a broad term that refers to a person who knows information without having a physical source of the knowledge, meaning they didn't use standard senses to achieve the knowledge. Throughout history these people have been known as fortune tellers and prophets. In the present day, a person might seek out a psychic to know whether their long lost lover will come back to them. But not all psychics are the same or do the same kind of work.

GHOSTLY GO-TO

While the term *medium* may have been used as early as the 1500s, *psychic* became more common in the late 1800s. The combined term *psychic medium* started to be commonly used in the later part of the 1900s.

The term *medium* often describes someone who can act as a mediator between the spirit world and the physical world. People most often seek out mediums to connect with those they knew in the physical world who have since passed into spirit. People might also connect with mediums to have a better understanding of the spiritual transition of one who has passed. Some mediums also specialize in higher spiritual frequencies or angelic connection. I believe mediums can work with a variety of different frequencies of spirits. It shouldn't be assumed that someone who refers to themself as a medium is only strictly connected to passed loved ones. Mediums are spiritual mediators, and when working with one you should ask them what frequency they specialize in.

In order to be a medium, a person must use psychic skills of perception. In order to be a psychic, a person must be able to connect with and mediate the spiritual connections the person in front of them has so that they may offer the necessary perceived message. This is why the two words are often interchangeable with one another. To say that you are one without the other often shows a lack of understanding of how spiritual communication works. That said, it does come down to what someone is most comfortable calling themself, which often has more to do with what kinds of beings they prefer to work with and how.

GHOSTLY GO-TO

Psychic mediums have used many different titles, such as shamans, prophets, diviners, oracles, and more. They have been spoken of since the beginning of civilization, culture, and social society.

Spiritual Practitioners

A spiritual practitioner is someone who not only is a psychic medium but also can reach into the spiritual plane and have an effect. For example, if someone is able to remove a spirit from a particular location, that makes them a spiritual practitioner. Assisting spirits in their own happiness and relieving spirits' uncertain feelings are also the work of the spiritual practitioner.

Unfortunately, there are some spiritual practitioners who take issue with psychic mediums. They may believe that the ability to speak to and understand sprits lower than deities is some kind of evil curse, or they may doubt that communication with spirits is possible. To the naysayers I ask, if you cannot pick up on spirits, how do you know if your work has been effective? Even talking to and receiving information from a higher being, such as a god, is by definition psychic mediumship. Be wary of anyone who uses spiritual practitioner abilities without understanding how those abilities can also work—both consciously and subconsciously—within everyone else. For example, if a priest performs a house blessing but has no way of knowing how to perceive spiritual energy within the house, how can he know whether his work is effective? Similarly, if a medium only works with one frequency and is called to cleanse a space where the frequency falls outside their specialty, they may miss the entity they came to work with. Spiritual practitioners need to be able to accurately perceive the energy they're working with in order to be effective; therefore, they must acknowledge and work on their psychic skill sets to carry out their work.

GHOSTLY GO-TO

In the late 1800s, "mediums" began to emerge as people who could contact spirits. Their over-the-top séances were immersive theatrical events with candles flickering to communicate spiritual answers, tables shaking to announce the presence of spirits, and mediums speaking for the deceased. These people earned psychic mediums a reputation as con artists—a stereotype that would last for decades to come.

Throughout this book I will refer to psychics, mediums, and spiritual practitioners somewhat interchangeably. However, as I aim to be as specific as possible, there may be some slight differentiations when I use the terms. For example, a psychic may pick up on information from the spirit world without always knowing which specific entity they're communicating with. Mediumship involves more specific spiritual communication, with knowledge of the spiritual being involved. To be a spiritual practitioner is to be able to work with said spirit or energy to create a change on the spiritual plane.

Psychic Medium Tools

Some mediums argue that the only way to connect with spirits is to purely channel them, without any outside tools whatsoever. And some say that psychics are more likely to use tools than mediums are. To those people, let me just say I prefer to give myself (and those learning with me) some slack. I come from the school of thought that believes that as long as it's coming from a credible source, validation is validation. Tools can often ground mediumship in objects of understanding in the here and now and on our plane. Why would you not utilize every skill and tool available to get the most effective and straightforward message possible? (I will discuss different types of tools that can be used to speak with spirits in Chapter 7.)

GHOSTLY GO-TO

As psychic mediumship has yet to be universally recognized or affirmed by science, there are not many official ways to be recognized as a verified spirit communicator. There are certainly pros and cons to this. One pro is that anyone who develops their skills can be a psychic medium. A major con is that the lack of formal certification makes some people unwilling to believe in the work psychic mediums do.

A Word about Psychic Bias

In mediumship, your psychic bias matters. Everyone has bias. It's best to be honest about it from the beginning, because bias will affect the way you understand what you experience. Your bias may come from a belief you have about the world around you. For example, some people believe that all ghosts are demons. Imagine a person who has this bias is approached by a ghost who's simply asking for directions. The person may immediately shield up, lose their cool, and think that a supposed demon is trying to possess them. Fear creates bias as well. In the animated Disney movie *Snow White*, the heroine runs into unfamiliar woods while fleeing for her life. She sees eyes all around her and begins to panic and cry. Once she allows herself a moment of calm, she realizes the eyes are those of friendly animals who don't actually mean her harm. Experiencing ghosts can be similar; if you're already scared, everything may come across as scary.

My bias is that spiritual energy will always be somewhere and that my role is to do my best to understand it—from the spirits' viewpoint, as well as from the perspective of my own experience and research. Your bias may come from a specific religious construct or a family viewpoint you were raised with. Bias is not always right or wrong. However, if you don't know your own bias, you're setting yourself up for confusion and disbelief. Be honest with yourself about what your psychic bias might be so you can understand it and how it affects the things you perceive.

As for me and what I teach? I just want to talk to ghosts. I don't feel like I have to constantly put specifications on who they are and why they're around as they are. I just talk to them and hope to learn something new. It's been working well for me so far, and millions of people have been appreciating my approach. And as like attracts like, I seem to regularly find myself in places with people who share the same sentiments.

For my personal preference, it is easier when I'm able to be with and meet ghosts with people who share my sentiments about perceptions. While I cannot always control who I work with in the field, I can control who I feel most comfortable with when exploring new places as a psychic medium. Having other open-minded people around who continue to search for answers and understanding as I do has helped me to shape how I go about meeting ghosts. It's a relief to be able to speak candidly with others about ghosts when we all are curious and supportive about the possibility of having new (and fun!) experiences, as you'll see in the next story.

GHOST STORY

SHARING PIE WITH GHOSTS . . .

If you're concerned about sharing your interest in ghosts with others, I would like to assure you that sometimes you just have to find yourself in the right location. Last year I was in Savannah, Georgia, for what's become something of an annual pilgrimage. As a kid I was just as terrified of Savannah as I was of ghosts. After all, the sprawling, actively growing port city has upheld a reputation as being one of the most haunted locations in the country. Once I finally visited Savannah as an adult, I could finally appreciate it for all that it was and has become—and since then, I've visited nearly every year.

As a unique treat, my partner, Tharyn (who is also a psychic medium), booked us a suite at Printmaker's Inn. The inn is a restored Victorian house, and staying there feels like staying in a living museum in the best ways. It was no surprise that as soon as we ascended the stairs to the second floor, we both picked up on not one but two very present spirits.

The first was a rather stern middle-aged woman whose dressing style seemed to fit the bill for the Edwardian era. Each time we even got close to the stairs, she was very clear that we should both hold the banister. Her attentiveness to those stairs was so keen that I began to wonder if she had witnessed a great trauma involving stairs at some point. Both Tharyn and I took to verbally announcing our caution whenever we found ourselves close to the stairs. Each time, this seemed to offer the poor woman a moment of calm.

The second spirit occupied a modern easy chair in the living area of the suite. He was a jovial sort of fellow whose clothing easily exceeded the age of the house. Naturally, this confused Tharyn and me at first, but we weren't about to tell the ghost that. We learned that houses in Savannah are commonly built on the sites of older houses, so we eventually concluded that it wasn't too surprising for a man from an earlier time to have wandered in at some point.

I took a moment to explain to the ghosts that Tharyn and I would be staying there for the next few days. Both spirits found that agreeable. Feeling confident about the possibility of learning their stories, I thanked them for speaking with me. Lastly, I told them we would be back later with a friend and would be happy to talk more.

After dinner, Tharyn and I and a local ghost tour guide and friend, Enocha, decided to pick up pie before walking back to the house. We popped into a little local shop called Pie Society where two women excitedly pointed out their personal favorites among the selection of pies.

Naturally, we had trouble deciding. I mentioned we'd be sharing the pie with the ghosts.

One of the workers enthusiastically asked, "Oh, you have ghosts?"

We explained where we were staying and told her about our experiences so far.

Without a second thought, the other worker said, "Then you have to take them pie too!"

The first worker nodded. "It's the polite thing to do. You don't want them to feel left out."

We all agreed and happily walked out with plenty of pie to share.

Did our offering of pie go over well? Absolutely! The woman was skeptical at first, but eventually she enjoyed a few bites of a coconut cream pie slice. The man was immediately enlivened and took almost the entire piece of chocolate silk pie. Besides perceiving these occurrences, we also observed how the pies' luster left them as the ghosts ate. The taste suddenly switched from decadent to dull; that's when we knew our offerings had worked.

We enjoyed getting to know the ghosts. We learned that the woman had come over after her home (next door) had been demolished. Her story was supported by historical information we learned from the owner the following day. Beneath her stoic exterior, the poor woman was sad about her home; she'd wound up at the inn after having nowhere else she felt she could go. The man who predated the house had entered the inn with a beauti-

ful antique clock that the owner had found at auction elsewhere in the state. The man seemed to be at ease in the house, and we made sure to let him have the big easy chair to himself. Our stay at the inn was very pleasant—all thanks to some open-minded Savannah locals and a few slices of pie.

IN SUMMARY

Spiritual energy of all frequencies and densities exists all around you to explore. If you find yourself holding any fear about spiritual events, I highly encourage you to remember that different frequencies and densities are neither good nor bad. In addition, you may or may not see ghosts, depending on where your focus is, and—for reasons that you should not take as personal slights—ghosts may or may not be drawn to you. It's important to steady yourself and focus on what brings you a sense of balance in your spiritual perception.

HERE ARE SOME KEY POINTS TO REMEMBER:

- A ghost is a piece of sentient memory—only a part of a soul.
- Spirits may move from place to place and from one frequency to another.
- High density does not equal bad or good, just as high-frequency vibration does not equal bad or good.
- Spirit, at any frequency or density, simply exists.
- You are in control of how you navigate all types of spirits.
- Not everyone will see or believe things as you do, as their biases may differ from yours.
- Not all psychic mediums have the same beliefs about the afterlife; beliefs differ based on bias, experience, and personal understanding.

CHAPTER 2

IS MY INTEREST IN THE PARANORMAL . . . NORMAL?

As you begin your journey toward building your psychic skills, it's important to first understand what you believe about spirits. Where did your paranormal curiosity come from? How did it grow? *Why* do you believe what you do? When you take the time to investigate what it is you believe, you lay a solid foundation from which to build your ghost communication skills without carrying fear or doubt into the process. You cannot begin to hone your psychic senses without this base of personal knowledge. In this chapter we'll talk about how to investigate what you and others believe about the paranormal in a not-so-scary way, while maintaining authenticity to yourself.

INVESTIGATING YOUR OWN BELIEFS ABOUT GHOSTS

It's important to understand how you personally developed an interest in the paranormal. Perhaps you grew up with an uncertain relationship with the spiritual. Or maybe you've seen a movie, read a book, or taken a ghost tour that made you wonder, *Is this real?* Regardless of how you became interested in the paranormal, it is important to understand what you believe you're looking at. There are a few ways to view this: through what you believe, through what others believe, and through your beliefs based on experiences. It's my hope that you consider all of those ways and create your own viewpoint of combined belief. Let's examine each one:

What You Believe

Even if you feel like you're in a place where you know *nothing* regarding spirits and the incorporeal plane, start with the idea that you know more than you think you do. Granted, you may not keep these same ideas and opinions over time, but it's better to start with something. If you find yourself having trouble assessing what you believe, start with the question *What if . . . ?* and go from there. To be clear, I don't mean to begin with a nonstarter such as *What if I'm wrong?* or *What if no one believes me?* Spiritual exploration is not about pleasing anyone else. It's about being honest and open with yourself. For now, there is nothing to prove. There is only you and the *What if . . . ?* For example:

- *What if* your ideas about the afterlife are valid?
- *What if* you know more than you thought you did?
- *What if* you could piece together an understanding that others also share and have had experiences with?
- *What if* ghosts don't have to be so scary if you only understood why they're around?

Write down your ideas. Keep in mind that these notes are only for you. You can always throw them away if you find something that contradicts them. The point of writing your ideas down is to help sort out what your thoughts are and to be able to read them back at a later time. You may be surprised later as what you learn through experience and research matches up with the beliefs you've recorded.

GHOSTLY GO-TO

You may find that some of your beliefs are based in a religious construct or even a fantastical one. That's okay! Write out whatever appeals to you, even if it's to say to yourself, *I would like this to be true, but for now I'm not sure.* You can also write out what you *don't* believe in to make it easier to identify what it is you *do* believe in.

If you're still having trouble figuring out what to ask yourself and where to start, here are some questions for you:

- What do or don't I believe happens after we die?
- What do I think a ghost is?
- What belief is that based on?
- Was that belief given to me, or was it personally experienced?
- Does exploring the paranormal feel safe to me? Why or why not?
- Am I open to changing my beliefs? Why or why not?
- Am I open to having more experiences with ghosts? Why or why not?

What Others Believe

The next step is to figure out what you *really* believe by challenging what you think you know. Keep in mind that the point of this exercise is not to cause overwhelm, doubt, or fear. The point is to better understand what resonates with you. When you listen to and try to understand what others believe, even if it's different from what you believe, you can gain critical thinking skills. Sadly, not everybody is open to being challenged in this way. When I was growing up in a Southern Baptist church, I was told I should never read another religion's holy books, as they might tempt me to shift my beliefs away from the Bible. What little faith they had in me! Having a natural curiosity about other beliefs and cultures is not a sin; rather, it's made me a far more rounded person. Through much research, talking with others, and travel, I've gained a steady understanding and sense of peace regarding my religious beliefs.

GHOSTLY GO-TO

Is it a little scary venturing out and asking others what they believe when you can't always back up what *you* believe with physical data? Sure. But what's worse—that fear, or sticking with old beliefs just because of the potential shame in learning a new truth? Understand that true steadiness is being able to listen to beliefs that are different from your own.

When you're considering what others believe about the paranormal and how they agree or disagree with your own views, it can be helpful to write down your thoughts and discoveries in a journal. Again, this free-flowing journal work is just for you, so feel free to write your feelings, doubts, and emotions as they pop up; no need to censor yourself. Here are some journal prompts to help you get started. Remember that your journey is your own! Use these questions as a jumping-off point for your further exploration:

- How do hauntings occur?
- Would a spirit want to stay behind?
  Why or why not?
- Has there ever been a ghost story you heard that you think has more to be discovered?
- What is the best part of being a ghost?
  The worst part?

- Are there subjects you would want to ask a ghost about that you wouldn't ask someone living about?

Take in what other people have written about the paranormal topics that interest you. Explore journals, research papers, magazines, blogs, social media channels, and so on. The point of this step is to explore the myriad opinions out there about the paranormal and the evidence people use to justify their claims. This is a time of research and deep diving. It's only through understanding what others believe that you can truly form your own opinions.

For example, as a kid, before I knew anything about how my own psychic abilities worked, I would watch mainstream media shows on spirits and sometimes get really confused. For example, a medium would come in, pick up on a ghost, and immediately want to move it on to "the light." In the show, I was being told ghosts had no place sharing this plane with us. I was told they were negative and even dangerous. However, I couldn't shake the feeling that ghosts were not all the same and that each experience could be different, just as each person is different. I allowed my views to be challenged and changed in some contexts, but I knew that what I was being fed wasn't quite right to me. Decades later, once I understood my abilities more, I began to hear and perceive that my theory was not just a theory. Through my own intuition, I'd had access to the truth the whole time.

GHOSTLY GO-TO

Catherine Crowe (1790–1872) may have been the first modern paranormal investigator. Her book *The Night-Side of Nature* brought the German-origin words *poltergeist* and *doppelgänger* into English usage.

Social media apps can be important places to practice discernment and clarify your personal beliefs. Algorithms that run on artificial intelligence are trained to show you subjects that will keep you hooked on apps. For example, if you continuously search for points that go against your beliefs and mainly interact by making a fuss in the comments sections of posts you disagree with, then when you search *ghosts* you may get a bunch of videos or articles that you hate. However, if you tend to interact by liking videos and leaving positive comments on content you agree with, your searches may result in materials more in line with what you believe in. If you'd like more of a general understanding of the topic you're researching, make a new account to do searches that aren't connected to your history on the app. To see just how much the algorithms are limiting what you see, I'd also encourage you to do some incognito searches online, try an entirely different search engine, or use a social media app that's new to you. Changing your IP address and perceived location can assist with this further.

Artificial intelligence (AI) tools also tend to tell you what you want to hear rather than what you need to hear. Using AI is not a good way to check your psychic readings or determine whether you're able to perceive spiritual activity. In my personal experience, I've known AI to be severely lacking when it comes to understanding the eccentricities of spirits. After all, chatbots and other AI tools simply work by imitating language that's been used elsewhere. They cannot speak with spirits and conceptualize what's happening—but *you* can. The way to learn about the spirit world is through experience, through checking that experience with others' readings, and by learning from whatever historical accounts you can find. AI cannot validate your experiences and knowledge for you.

GHOSTLY GO-TO

When looking at sources that offer little credibility, such as some influencers and/or bloggers, always check in with yourself and your beliefs. Ask if what they're saying resonates with you, and then ask yourself, *Why or why not?* If you realize your respect for someone's statements is based on their popularity/following, ask yourself why that's important. Remember: Popularity, entertainment value, and sensationalism do not always equal experience.

When I first started answering people's questions on social media, I did not consider myself a psychic medium. What's even more wild to me is that no one ever asked me *how* I knew what I knew when I answered their questions about ghosts. Looking back, I wish they had, because it may have allowed me to figure out a few important things about myself. I have a passion for learning, and so I began to connect with other spiritually sensitive creators and some local psychics in my area. I asked them many questions on their experiences with spirits. I kept pursuing answers. I manifested the right people to come across my path so that I could learn as effectively and efficiently as possible. Were all the people who were put in my path those I resonated with? Absolutely not! In fact, I went through a few years of highly confident and truly terrible teachers. However, learning what *didn't* resonate with me allowed me to better understand what *did*—and to find others who shared those resonant qualities.

Remember: The purpose of seeking out others' beliefs is to both challenge and affirm your own. Sometimes that may leave you feeling validated; other times it may leave you feeling angry or upset. But all of these experiences will help you shape and strengthen your own beliefs. Stay curious.

Belief Through Experience

As with anything in life, personal belief is built upon the experiences you have. This is as true with the spiritual as it is with the physical. For example, part of what you decide to believe may be based on the ghost stories you've heard from others around you. If you've already experienced something paranormal, you may explain your encounter using the best knowledge you have, until further information comes to you and changes how you see that experience. Your beliefs may also be shaped by comparing your paranormal encounters with other people's experiences and with the history of a location.

Do you have to start with journaling your thoughts and reading research papers before you go out to experience hauntings? Of course not! While the preceding sections propose a certain order of events for exploring your beliefs, growth is seldom linear. For example, I was experiencing paranormal encounters and listening to others' beliefs way before I ever started asking myself what my own beliefs were. Would I recommend you explore your own beliefs and research what other people have said on the topic before you go out and try to communicate with ghosts? Of course. However, if you were drawn to reading this book, I imagine you may have already experienced something supernatural in your life, so obviously this exact order may not work for everyone.

While I'll be providing more considerations for going to haunted locations later, I would first like to give you a piece of advice: Go in ready to be surprised. Allow yourself to learn. Keep your mind open to contradiction. Stay curious. Just because someone else had a specific experience with a specific entity, that doesn't mean that the same is meant for you. You are not them. The past may or may not repeat itself. Always first connect with your own beliefs about what is for you to experience.

GHOSTLY GO-TO

As much as we would like to pretend we're always in control of the world around us, we're not. Ghosts will do as they do. The living will have thoughts and feelings about it. You will need to figure out where you fit into that. That said, you do not need to be a pushover when going out to experience hauntings. If something doesn't feel right—incorporeal or physical—you do not need to stay.

Remember that being intuitive isn't about getting everything right every time. Neither is it about exhaustive repetition of events that have happened to others. Rather, being intuitive is about finding yourself where it's best for you to be, rather than where you may have thought you ought to be. Life is about the journey, not the destination. We're meant to travel and explore and learn. Put yourself in the mindset to find what it is *you* need to find.

Combining Beliefs

Once you've considered others' beliefs and identified your own, it will be necessary to combine all that you've learned to come to a better understanding of spiritual possibilities. This just comes down to understanding what resonates best with *you*. You may feel that a location and the gender of a ghost you researched resonate with the personal, intuitive feelings you experienced at the same spot. Or you may have had a feeling a place was not haunted, only to find a story of someone else's experience there and choose to believe in that possibility. Over time, both researched experience and your beliefs about what is possible will influence your personal understanding.

Throughout your research, it will be important to revisit your beliefs and reflect on them. Ask yourself the hard questions. Really feel what resonates with you in your gut. It's okay to write things like, *I really feel X is true, but I've yet to find it*. It's important to state the intentions you have for yourself. After all, everything is a hypothesis until it can be tested. And yes, the scientific method can be applied to haunted experiences. Here's a simplified example:

Observation: You observe and/or feel a paranormal experience.

Question: You ask yourself, *Was that a ghost?*

Hypothesis: If the experience can be replicated without physical manipulation, it may be a ghost.

Experiment: Repeat the steps that led up to the paranormal encounter to the best of your ability.

Analysis: If you or someone else is able to replicate the haunting and there is still no physical explanation for the event, the location may be haunted.

Conclusion: Based on the experiences, research, and experiments implemented, the location may hold a probability of being haunted.

GHOSTLY GO-TO

Make the process of exploring and combining your beliefs as much fun as possible. If it ever feels like work, that's an indication to explore what's making it feel that way—not a reason to stop exploring or, worse, to trudge through the process with disdain and bitterness. Spiritual growth can always be put down and picked back up again. All you need to do is set the intention of interest, mean what you say, and expect that the right thing will be put in your path and will motivate you to pull out your notes again.

It's possible that you may conclude you experienced ghostly activity, even if you didn't realize what you were experiencing in real time. Sometimes you may need to recall events to check them against the experiences of others who are more versed in the paranormal event. That can be a valid way to implement combining your beliefs with others'. Here's a story of how this happened to me.

GHOST STORY

THE RESIDENT WOMAN

Well before I understood myself as spiritually sensitive, I found myself with a group of randomly assembled acquaintances in the lobby of the Biltmore Greensboro Hotel. This building in downtown Greensboro, North Carolina, has a rich history, having been both a prominent office building and an inn at different times during its over one hundred years of existence. One of the members of the group knew an employee who worked as a nighttime lobby attendant. It was a very slow night at the hotel, and many of the rooms were vacant. Knowing that the group of us were there for paranormal lore, the employee offered to show us around and tell us tales of the haunted historic building.

As we made our way up to the second floor, I began to feel goosebumps on my neck and back. The entire group was looking to be scared, and I was entertained by their

excitement but was otherwise focused on the interesting possibility of encountering a ghost. We entered a quaint room that was painted pink. Once our small group was inside, the employee held the door open and told us to watch. She then let go of the door, and it slowly shut on its own.

"This is the only hotel room where the door always shuts itself," she told us. "We have checked for drafts, weight, and imbalance. Nothing physical has been able to explain why this door shuts. We believe it's because of Lydia."

We were then told the tragic tale of a young sex worker who met her end at the hand of one of her customers. The employee told us that Lydia took care of the room and would turn on the sink from time to time. Whether she was trying to communicate something or just trying to wash her face was up to interpretation. The staff acknowledged the spirit whenever applicable, and they regularly let her know she was welcome to stay as long as she didn't upset guests.

As I listened to the story of poor Lydia, I found myself staring into the mirror across from the double beds. My eyes relaxed and became unfocused. Behind me, I could almost make out the transparent shape of someone a bit taller than me. The shape looked light blue-green to me. A heat rose up my back, and I felt as if someone were standing directly behind me. I had always been told ghosts were cold, so feeling someone warm confused me. I wanted to believe it was Lydia saying hello, but I felt like what I was experiencing made no sense. As the group prepared to leave the room, I brushed off the feeling and moved on.

Later that night, we all found ourselves in the lobby again. The employee shared some more stories about some of the ghosts that guests and staff had encountered. When the conversation came to a natural end and others began to talk amongst themselves, I took the chance to talk to the employee privately. I explained what I'd seen and described the heat that I'd felt while in Lydia's room, and I asked if any of it made sense to her. The employee nodded and said that Lydia has oftentimes been associated with warmth—by a variety of different guests, psychic mediums, and paranormal investigators.

Even though the experience with Lydia may have been small, I felt so validated. I had gone into the experience believing that ghosts were always cold. I had an experience that challenged that belief, and then I found out that the same sensation had been felt more than once by other people. It's been over ten years, and I've yet to make it back to the Biltmore Greensboro. Should I find myself up in Lydia's room again, I will be sure to give her a personal thank-you for wanting to connect with me that night.

Doubt Is Normal

As you examine your belief system and build a new one, you may experience the Dunning-Kruger effect. It goes like this: At first, when you're gaining new skills and understanding, you may feel very excited and confident with all you're doing. You jump in. You're thrilled about all that you've learned already and all that you're able to do. But then, over time, as you learn even more, you begin to realize you don't know nearly as much as you thought you did. You may get down on yourself during this period. Even though your knowledge has increased, you may feel *more* insecure or incompetent than you did when you knew much less. You're more aware of—and discouraged by—all that you still have left to learn. This is the stage where many people give up.

The good news is the Dunning-Kruger effect comes to an end as your awareness fluctuates. In time, having grown through doubts and discouragement, you can rise into true well-rounded competence. You know what you're capable of. You've experienced hardship, but you've worked through that rock-bottom feeling. Your confidence is no longer out to prove itself; rather, it's quiet. Your confidence is secure and aligned with your actual knowledge and skill.

GHOSTLY GO-TO

Psychologists David Dunning and Justin Kruger first described the Dunning-Kruger effect in 1999. They discovered that performers lacking metacognition in a particular subject often believed they were much more proficient than they actually were.

You can see my own experience with the Dunning-Kruger effect in my social media journey. When I started out in 2019, I miraculously had all the answers. I felt *so* capable as a creator. Once I started to provide psychic mediumship services to people in 2021, I began to realize that while I thought I knew a lot, I had barely scratched the surface of all there was to know about ghosts. People came into my life who had years of experience beyond mine—people who spoke with so much more authority than me. I fell into discouragement.

By 2023 I felt as if I was constantly trying to prove myself. I had a passion for teaching, and I wanted people to believe in themselves, but really what I was lacking was belief in myself. I'd had so many incredible psychic experiences with the living and dead alike, and yet I was still trying to overcome the insecurities I had developed when my abilities were challenged. It wasn't until 2025 that I finally let the things I couldn't change go and began to sit on the other side of the Dunning-Kruger effect. Now, when I'm challenged with something that doesn't resonate with me, I can more easily shrug and say, "That wasn't my experience, but people are welcome to believe as they like."

As you move forward on your spiritual journey you may feel flashes of doubt and uncertainty. You may feel like you're progressing well and then be stuck with feelings of skepticism or failure. Just know that this is normal. Everyone learning a new skill goes through a similar period. Don't let these feelings dissuade you from your paranormal explorations. The doubt is merely a normal stage. Persevere through it to come out improved on the other side.

INVESTIGATING YOUR PAST EXPERIENCES

If you have your own life experiences with the paranormal to unpack, when you're ready, there's no time like the present to do so. Revisiting those experiences might mean revisiting some scary moments that feel very much out of your control. Keep in mind that, even if the frightening event happened relatively recently, you're not the same person you were when you first experienced it. Mark how different you are now from then. You may be older; you may be with or without different people in your immediate life; you may even be in a different location.

Treat the present-day you as a mentor to your past self. Rather than seeing the event first-hand all over again, look at it from outside of yourself. Here are a few ideas for how to do this:

- Maybe you'd like to choose to see the event as if you were watching yourself on a television screen.
- Maybe past-you would like to tell present-you the experience as though you were a trusted friend. Imagine this private conversation.
- Perhaps you could write out a conversation between your past and present self—in the form of a play or a script—to better ground yourself.

Once you've listened to the story your past self shared, ask yourself what it is you know now that you didn't know then. Did something in your life shift before the event? What changed after the event? Does your experience match with any other paranormal experiences you've been able to find through research? Really deconstruct your understanding, even if it's just an acknowledgment of the aspects you still do not understand.

If at any point you find yourself slipping into fear about the event, take a moment to remind yourself that you are your own ally and you are in control of your own protection. You can always put your explorations down and come back to them later. You can always talk over your experience with a friend or even a mental health professional.

Understanding psychic perception often requires looking back at events and how your body and mind reacted to them. A single happening may seem so small, you might not be ready to call it a psychic encounter; however, over time, if you regularly experience the same feeling following a repeated event, you may start to see that experience as a haunting. What significantly helped me realize I was picking up on spiritual activity was living in a house with a regimented and routine-oriented spirit.

GHOST STORY

GERTY AND THE GHOST BUS STOP HOUSE

The first house I toured when moving to Wilmington, North Carolina—a house where I would end up living for over a year and a half—had a plethora of spirits passing through it at any given time due to its location: It was the center point between three unmarked burial grounds. The key figure who kept all the comings and goings of spirits—alive and dead—in line was an elderly lady I nicknamed Gerty.

As I toured the home the spirit of a woman followed a respectful distance behind me. How did I know that? I didn't, really. It was just a feeling I kept shoving away. I felt her presence. I wished I could see her with my eyes to somehow prove to myself that my feeling was real, but it took a while for my eyes to catch up.

As I moved into that house, I began to feel a sort of disdain whenever I looked at all my unpacked boxes. While I do consider myself a tidy person, I usually give myself some grace as long as nothing is in the way of day-to-day function. However, whenever I passed the boxes, especially those that piled up in the common areas, I couldn't help but feel disdain and judgment.

How strange! I didn't feel like I was judging myself, but I could still feel a heavy feeling all around me. Words permeated my thoughts: *Clean this up. Put that away.* Yet, the thoughts didn't feel like my own. I had lived in much worse conditions and with far more roommates in the past. I didn't feel like I needed to be so hard on myself, but the words and feelings continued.

Hardly a month into living in the house, things came to a head when I could sense the woman standing right behind me in the hall leading to the front living room. Without thinking, I quickly moved and turned to face the corner where I felt she was standing, even though I couldn't see her. "I'll do it this week. Compromise, okay? Just stop making me feel bad!"

A feeling of shock came from the corner I'd directed my words to. Slowly, the feeling backed away. I could almost see her leave the room. I kept my word. The feeling faded. That was my first understanding of how Gerty wanted her house kept. To be fair, she had a point about the boxes. However, there was a second issue Gerty and I disagreed about, and on this one I was not going to back down.

As my dog, Mira, and I moved in and began to spend time in the house, I couldn't seem to get the words *Dogs belong outside* out of my head! I knew the words weren't mine. Mira had always been an inside dog. I ignored the words that kept popping into my mind.

On the first rainy day we were living there, Gerty became very upset. Mira was never a fan of rain or water. She knew to do her business outside, but on rainy days that took a lot of coaxing to accomplish. Trying to give her a little something to do, I took to throwing her rope toy down the hall for her to fetch. While Mira was all too happy to have somewhere to put her energy, Gerty was horrified.

Dogs belong outside echoed in my mind until even the room seemed darker somehow. I felt Gerty nearby like she was shouting in my ear. I finally believed what was happening when, running back to me with the rope toy in her mouth, Mira looked up at me and then looked to something *next to* me. My dog's eyes widened and then narrowed. Her posture changed and she whined. I knew I wasn't making it up.

Sighing, I finally explained to the presence near me, "She doesn't live outside. She's afraid of thunderstorms and hates being wet. I know you don't like dogs, but this is something I won't compromise on. But I promise to always clean her feet before she comes in. She's a good dog. You'll see."

I could feel Gerty huff. We stood off with each other for a few seconds. Mira's whimper broke the tension, and as I walked toward my dog to comfort her, Gerty walked in the opposite direction. Two different experiences in less than a two-week period of living in the house. It was Gerty who inspired me to really begin to dig into communicating with ghosts. If there was going to be peace, we would have to work together.

Once we came to an understanding, Gerty was less pointed about Mira being in the house. While Gerty never seemed to appreciate Mira for being the lovable potato she was, I picked up on less curt remarks from her.

From time to time Gerty would glare at Mira from across the room, but everyone, including Mira, stopped being bothered by it over time. As long as I was sure to keep the furniture and floors clean of dog hair and dirt, Gerty eventually accepted a dog being in the house.

INVESTIGATING OTHERS' EXPERIENCES

In my time talking to clients, commenters, workshoppers, and beyond, the number one conflict people bring up is that they don't have an immediate way to explore spiritual experiences. Some are too busy to visit historic places that have known ghosts. Others, due to previous bad experiences, are too afraid to venture out. The good news is it's always possible to pursue an understanding of spirits through someone else's experience.

Media

When I was first starting my spiritual reawakening, I turned to forms of media for inspiration and information. Fortunately, there were a plethora of movies, books, and television shows at the time to pick from. I first picked the media that felt the least scary to me. I asked myself if what I was watching and absorbing felt possible. Then I asked myself, *Why or why not?* I journaled on what might have inspired the writers, actors, and directors. I researched any interviews I could find. Art and media are fantastic sources of spiritually inspired thought.

GHOSTLY GO-TO

The 1896 French short film *Le Manoir du Diable* (*The House of the Devil*), directed by George Méliès, is said to have been the first horror movie. Méliès is celebrated for his illusions and special effects. The original film is about three minutes long and can be found online.

When taking in media about spirits, I look for traces of elements that connect with my personal experiences. For example, the 2013 movie *The Conjuring* was incredibly impactful for me because it showed a medium who could see spiritual energy behind people. That absolutely resonated with my experience! Is that to say the entire movie matched up? Not at all; for example, I've yet to see a creepy clown figure hanging over a wardrobe. Sometimes you have to take what works and release what doesn't.

The 2018 Netflix television series *The Haunting of Hill House* resonated with me on many levels, most specifically by showing the hardship a family can endure when a haunting is pulling them apart. The movies *The Others* (2001) and *The Sixth Sense* (1999) showed the reality of ghosts getting lost, forgetting how they got there—and how terrifying that can be. Even Disney's *Coco* (2017) has elements of ghosts, ancestors, and spiritual connection that I found easy to understand and relatable. When I started to look at these media sources as ways to connect with and better understand my own beliefs, suddenly they were not nearly as scary.

Social Media Stories

The sky is the limit whenever you begin to research ghost stories online. Reddit, TikTok, and YouTube are all filled with people's wild experiences. I encourage you to keep your sense of critical thinking engaged whenever you read or watch them. Even if a person's story is entirely true to them, that doesn't mean it has to be something you absorb and use for your own awareness. If you find yourself getting too afraid, take a moment to ground yourself. Remember that your research is about learning. Scares can be fun in their place and time, but not when you're trying to simply understand your beliefs. Keep a level head.

You may also feel moved to share your own stories on social media and ask for the perspectives of others. This is how I got started on what soon would eventually become the Rebekah The Ghost Guide channels. In my stories, I was honest about not fully understanding what I was seeing or experiencing. Sometimes people would comment with ideas that were thought-provoking. Other times people contributed fearful responses that were neither beneficial to my understanding nor logical.

To this day, some of my favorite comments are from people who say that they don't know if they believe me but they enjoyed my stories. Perfect! I do not put information out there to make people change their understanding. However, what I do love is when my story is captivating enough for someone to listen, watch, and imagine their own resourceful what-if scenarios. While there are certainly scary things out there, I don't aim to frighten; rather, I aim to understand.

FINDING PEACE WITH WHAT YOU BELIEVE

Now that you've examined what you believe, challenged it against what others believe, and formed a new, more well-rounded set of combined beliefs, it's important to take a minute and find peace with what you have learned. Remember: Belief starts with the self. No one is expected to know everything about where we end up—and why—once our mortal coils expire. However, there is something to be said about coming to peace with your own view of the afterlife—even if your peace rests on the decision to not believe anything happens at all.

You may find your peace in organized religion. There are many religions, and they hold a variety of beliefs about spiritual frequencies and what happens after death. You may decide to adhere to a religion's larger concepts but allow yourself to accept your psychic perceptions as truths that fall outside of the religion's preconceived understanding.

Or you may choose a route of your own design. You may make your own way without a stated set of beliefs. Whatever route you choose, please know that you can reroute at any time. You can believe multiple things at once—or nothing at all. The point is that you start this spiritual journey with whatever sense of peace you need to be able to relax and explore.

IN SUMMARY

You'll need to come to terms with your own beliefs while also being flexible enough to allow them to change so that you don't get caught in a corner of fear and insecurity. In spiritualism, you're meant to come up with your own conclusions. You want to be sure you're letting yourself grow in your own understanding—while never allowing your morals to become corrupted by beliefs that don't align with you.

HERE ARE SOME KEY POINTS TO REMEMBER:

- Utilize *What if* when you sort your theories.
- Prepare to learn about opinions that may either oppose or validate your own.
- It's okay to adjust your beliefs.
- Be aware of the Dunning-Kruger effect.

CHAPTER 3

UNDERSTANDING YOUR ENERGY

In order to successfully communicate with ghosts, you must first be aware of your own energy. Understanding your energy (and how to keep it clean) not only makes you feel better and more confident in yourself; it can also keep you safe from entities that may not have the best intentions for you. In this chapter, you'll learn how crucial it is to be mindful of the energy you are presenting. You'll also create powerful statements that will help you feel relaxed and mindful and—beyond that—will give you a positive bump to see yourself as the superhero you are.

START WITH YOURSELF: WHY IT'S IMPORTANT TO BE AWARE OF YOUR OWN ENERGY

One of the biggest rookie mistakes you can make as a spiritually sensitive person is to skip checking in with your own energy. At a minimum, this oversight may lead you to put your own bias on a situation you're reading, rather than allowing the pure read to come through. Worse, if you're unaware of your own energy, you might subconsciously call to the negative energy you already have—and create a larger spiritual issue, either for yourself or for the place you're in.

Unfortunately, many psychic mediums have fallen into the trap of projecting their own thoughts and feelings onto the spirits they're encountering. When mediums do not first check in with themselves to understand their own psychic biases and how their personal feelings of imbalance may affect their readings, their spiritual mediations may come back askew. (For more on biases, see Chapter 1.) For example, say a particular medium believes that spirits suddenly know everything after death, that they have no pain (not even emotional pain), and that they're no longer susceptible to enjoying physical vices. If this medium sees a spirit smoking, they may either block that detail out completely (affecting the validity of their reading) or decide the spirit is somehow evil for enjoying a cigarette after death. The medium projects their own mental blocks and personal beliefs onto the spirit, rather than allowing the spirit to exist as themself. A medium who feels they have little control and safety in their everyday life might misread a haunted spot in a different way—they might feel as if every ghost is out to hurt them. While we're all human and are capable of mistakes, this book will provide you the tools you need to avoid creating inaccurate projections.

Good spiritual hygiene and a strong shield (more on that later) will not only protect you from any spirits that may mean you harm but also help you to better understand yourself. Just as physical hygiene starts with understanding when to wash your hands and how to avoid illness, spiritual hygiene starts with understanding the energy of your soul and how to keep your spirit clean. The good news is this process does not have to be time-consuming, and the better you understand the energy within you, the faster the process will be. Most importantly, taking care of your spiritual hygiene can be a fun refresh! The following is the story of a time when my lack of mindfulness about my spiritual hygiene caused trouble in my life:

GHOST STORY

GERTY VERSUS A NEGATIVE ENTITY I BROUGHT HOME

It had already been a long day: My family was in town, my partner at the time and I had gotten into yet another fight, and I also happened to be living in the most haunted house on the street. Once I got my family settled at our place, I headed down to the river to lead a ghost tour. My energy was gross. I hadn't shielded; in the rush of everything, I had forgotten to. Some of the guests on

the tour were pressing me to tell super-scary stories. It was a perfect setup for disaster.

The tour that day included the typical spots: a marked burial ground, an unmarked burial ground, the oldest house in town, and so on. I didn't have the mental capacity to think that anything might be following me. Sure, it had happened before—at a time when I had more wits about me. On this day, my stress and my lack of spiritual awareness combined with the mental ache of an upset relationship and the stress of playing host to family created a perfect storm of issues.

When I returned home after the tour, my house felt darker than usual. Everything seemed on edge. I thought it had to do with the awkwardness my family felt about the messy situation with my then-partner. I knew the house was haunted. I knew the ghosts didn't appreciate our bickering and were skeptical of new people staying in the house. I knew about all these factors, but it never crossed my mind that something malicious had used my energy to walk right through the front door.

With our argument unresolved, I had scooted as far away from my boyfriend as possible and fell asleep tired and angry. Then the nightmares came. I felt held down, as if an unseen blanket had been thrown over my body and was keeping me still. I woke up unable to move. Fear permeated the room. I willed my body to move. I thought if I could only wake up my boyfriend, I might feel a little better. That's when I heard a voice in my mind:

He doesn't care about you.

Those words hurt, yes. But then I thought of my dog sleeping just on the other side of the room. I could hear her whimpering in her sleep. Was she having a nightmare too? Next to me, my boyfriend also started to wince and turn in his sleep. I wanted to at least wake my dog. I knew she could make me feel better.

She won't hear you.

I began to fight panic. I couldn't speak. I started to think out a plea for anyone to help. I just needed some-one—anyone—to be there with me. If only someone could wake up and turn on a light, I knew I could figure out what was going on.

The room became even darker. A shadow passed across the wall.

It was right then that the smoke detector began to scream.

Naturally, it woke up the entire house. Lights turned on all around. My boyfriend began to fan the device. Even though there was no smoke in the room and, oddly, the detector just on the other side of the door was not going off, the alarm continued to wail. My boyfriend eventually had to rip the batteries out to get it to stop.

After a few moments of collective confusion, we soon found out that *everyone* had been having nightmares and so welcomed the alarm, even though it was three o'clock in the morning. I knew something was up. There were too many coincidences. But if a malicious entity had entered the house, why would it give itself away by setting off

the alarm? Thinking it through, I realized that someone *else* must have been responsible for the racket that woke us all from our nightmares: the most prominent house ghost, Gerty.

While I didn't fully know or understand how I was perceiving energy at the time, I did what I could to connect with Gerty using a pendulum. I realized she was furious that I had brought something so awful into the house. She heard my silent cries in the night and did what she had to do. I thanked her and apologized profusely. As soon as the sun came up, I smoke cleansed that thing out of the house and sent it back to the burial ground it had come from.

All of this could have been avoided if, before that tour, I had merely checked in with my own energy to ensure I wasn't subconsciously calling out for something malicious to tag along.

PROACTIVE PROTECTION

Using the experience in the previous ghost story, let's break down how logic and psychic perception can be in or out of balance. All things considered, I was being fairly logical about what was causing the weird feelings in my home that day. I thought that my issues had been of my own making. I didn't initially think that my experiences had to do with spirits, because they didn't. The stress of hosting family, the challenges of work, and the tension of relationship issues were aspects of my day that were not spiritual. Because of this, I figured my insecurities and my situation were my own to sort out. However, that logical explanation for my distress should not have been an excuse to forgo my basic spiritual protections. As I later learned, I should have seen the physical and emotional stress of the day as a reason to *amp up* my protections.

GHOSTLY GO-TO

Research suggests that our brains may produce an evolutionarily rooted fear of the dark. This is often thought to exist as a way to keep us safe from nocturnal predators. As a result, light has a positive effect on the amygdala, the region of the brain involved in fear conditioning.

This is where my "why not" philosophy regarding spiritualism and practitioner work comes into effect. Had my day been made stressful by my own choices in ways that had little to do with ghosts? Yes. Would I have slept more soundly if I had gotten ahead of my protections? Absolutely. So, *why not* smoke cleanse before entering the house, just as a precaution? *Why not* put on some extra protective jewelry before leaving for my ghost tour? *Why not* say a prayer to my protective guides, even during the stresses? Many things can be done that allow for proactive protection.

In the next chapter I will break down different ways that you can shield yourself, but for the purposes of this chapter, I want you to first understand your own energy—and how to keep it clean from anything that may not have the best of intentions toward you.

GROUNDING YOUR ENERGY THROUGH MINDFULNESS

Grounding your energy is how you stay connected to yourself no matter what spiritual or psychic information you may be getting. Mindfulness is the foundation of the grounding process. Mindfulness teaches you to start with yourself and your own energy before you journey into anything outside of yourself. The good news is this process doesn't have to be a fully drawn-out hour-long ordeal. You just need to get a better understanding of what your energy feels like when balanced, and then you can move forward from there. There are many ways you can pursue grounded mindfulness. I would encourage you to find what works best for you. The first option is not always the quick fix! Sometimes you might need to try a few different ways to figure out your own best method.

Claim Your Own Energy

Claiming your own energy is one of the most basic and important steps you can take to ground your energy. A simple statement will do; here are a few examples for your consideration:

My energy is my own. Only that which I allow may connect with me.

I am in control of my body, mind, and spirit. Only I control my choices and actions.

Only that which means me well may make contact with my energy. I claim only my energy as my own.

These are only a few examples; you should make your own statements that feel right to you. As you say the words, allow them to bring you a sense of peace and balance and maybe even a touch of badassery. After all, you are your own hero. You want to speak and/or think words to yourself that remind you just how awesome you are. Depending on where you are with your mental health journey, this may take some practice. That said, the only way to start is to start.

GHOSTLY GO-TO

Mindfulness techniques have been proven to reduce stress, anxiety, and depression by positively stimulating the prefrontal cortex and amygdala. Mindfulness leads to improved emotional regulation, self-awareness, feelings of resilience, and mental concentration.

Mindful Techniques

In preparing to take a good long look at yourself, you may feel you need a little bit of help. That's entirely okay! Mindfulness is not a competition. Do whatever it is you need to do to be able to concentrate. It's important to understand what *relaxed*, *cozy*, and *safe* mean for you. You may like to try different methods of loosely structured and relaxing activities to create a good, safe feeling for yourself. Here are a few examples of tools and actions that may help your brain to calm down:

- Drawing
- Walking
- Gazing out a window
- Spending time in nature
- Handcrafts (knitting, crochet, diamond art, painting, and so on)
- Binaural beats/sound waves
- Calming music
- White, pink, green, or brown noise
- Noise-canceling headphones
- Fidget toys
- Eye mask and/or earplugs
- Cozy blanket
- Herbal tea
- Fuzzy socks
- Calming imagery

At the very least, you want to make sure that your brain has the option to relax. If you need to simply focus on what relaxed feels like to you, start there. Having thoughts cross your mind is simply your subconscious trying to remind you of what you feel is most important. Gently remind your brain that you do not need to do anything else or be anywhere else but where you are. If it helps, keep a notepad nearby to jot down things that come up in your thoughts so that you can get them out of your brain and focus back on yourself.

Mindfulness Is Not Always a Linear Process

Personally, the beginning of my mindfulness meditations often looks a little frazzled. I have to figure out what sitting comfortably feels like to me at any given time. I usually have a flurry of thoughts come to the front of my mind. I write them down and then gently tell my brain thanks for the reminder and that I'll get to those things later. Sometimes meditation is a little like gentle parenting for your brain. It can be natural to want to bark at your thoughts to calm down, but that does not create calm. Aim for kindly understanding yourself, as you would a friend coming to you for help. Remind your brain and body that you're safe and in control of your thoughts and feelings.

Understand that meditating is not always a linear process. You don't have to go straight into complete stillness without looking back; it's okay to jot down thoughts and reposition your body if that's what you need to do. If you find yourself getting sleepy, that's okay too. In fact, if you stay awake but feel sleepy, that's your mind slipping into what's called theta state. When our brains are in theta state, we're able to channel psychic information, and everyone can gain the ability to slip in and out of theta state throughout the day. I will explain more about theta state in Chapter 5, but for now, simply understand that relaxation is a state of inner awareness rather than outer awareness. It's the inner awareness you want to focus on for now.

HOW TO DO A BODY SCAN

If you've tried to relax and be mindful and have tried to claim your own energy with your statement and it still doesn't feel authentic, you may need to do a body scan to better understand where your energy is at. You should start this process slowly and really give your energy your undivided attention. Once you know your energy well, the process will become quicker. Whether this scan first takes you one minute or ten, it's better to do *something* to understand your energy rather than nothing at all. Understanding how to scan your body will be the foundation of the psychic energy checks that you will learn about later.

Step One: The Physical Check-In

Take a breath. Allow the exhalation to really affect your physical body. Let your shoulders drop. Relax your jaw and let your tongue drop too. Do a little shake if you feel your arms, torso, or legs are storing any kind of energy that feels heavy or dense. Hop a little bit if you can. Let the tension fall into the floor. Take another breath. Laugh if you need to. It's okay to feel silly. None of this has to be too serious if you don't want it to be. All that matters is that you're releasing anything that may keep you from connecting with *you*.

GHOSTLY GO-TO

Jumping has been psychologically proven to emit mood-boosting endorphins that improve cognitive function and reduce stress. Jumping or even just shaking the shoulders can increase blood flow and help more oxygen reach the brain.

Once you've shaken out anything that isn't serving you, take a more centering breath. Allow that breath to really reach the bottom of your lungs. If it helps to put a hand over your gut to ensure that your breath is really getting down there, do that. Repeat as needed at whatever pace works for you. Focus on how the breath moves in and out. Acknowledge that your body and mind work together to do this all the time, with or without your thinking about it. Be present in the understanding that you can do great things without even having to think about them. Let trust carry you past any insecurities or self-doubt that may pop up. Trust that you know exactly what to do and when to do it.

Step Two: The Soul Energy Check-In

In this step you'll utilize your inner eye. If you happen to have aphantasia (meaning you're unable to see visuals in your mind's eye), *speak* to your mind instead. See or understand what your body looks like before you. Pretend you're looking into a mirror or having your reflection spoken back to you.

Rather than focusing on your physical features, ask yourself, *What does my soul energy look like?* Your soul energy is the energy that is the source of your body's cognizance, movement, and thought. Is there a color? Texture? Sound? Smell? Focus on the parts of you that are interesting. Is there flow? Any interesting glow? Where? Why do you think that is? Simply mull over the possibilities. There are no wrong answers here. After all, it's your energy. Trust that you know it best. Trust that you know how, where, and why your energy flows as it does.

If you find yourself getting distracted from being able to see, understand, and ask these energetic questions about yourself, it's time to pull that image into the physical. Get out a piece of paper and draw a basic body outline of yourself and what the energy looks like to you. If more colorful visuals help you to better understand yourself, then pull out the colored pencils (or whatever it is you have on hand). If the idea of a big, colorful art project excites you, go for it! If that feels intimidating, then start with just using a pen and a scrap of paper to get it done. Remember that this work is different for every individual. What works for one person might not work for another.

Once you've done whatever's needed to see your energy, it's time to look for any areas that don't seem to flow the same way the rest of your energy does. For myself, I might sense areas where my energy moves in wavy lines—but then suddenly notice another area where stagnant energy shows up as crumpled or spiky lines. If you're more color oriented, maybe your energy mainly appears as your favorite color but turns to your least favorite in a particular area. Ask yourself if there's a way to bring the flowing energy into the area of stagnant energy. This doesn't have to be hard. If an easy answer comes up (*Open a door* or *Just wave it over*), do it! You might envision the changing in your mind, move the energy with your hands, or draw out what should happen. If it feels a little like you're making it up, just go with it and have fun. Your imagination is your friend here.

GHOSTLY GO-TO

The placebo effect is a psychological phenomenon where a person perceives a physical change without physical treatment. It is estimated to occur in one out of every three people. As long as the effect proves quantifiably positive, I see this as a testament to the brain's ability to heal the body without relying on anything further than belief.

Step Three: The Soul Energy Examination

The next step of your body scan acknowledges your own energy as well as any energy around you that you may not find useful. During Step 2, you may have already noticed some areas where the energy just didn't seem to be your own. For example, say you saw a hole in your energy somewhere, or you noticed something that looked like a spindly root. Follow that image in your mind. Ask yourself, *Is that a connection worth keeping? Why or why not?* Let your thoughts about the energy travel to the front of your consciousness. You may not need to do anything about them at present; however, you should know and acknowledge what is connected to your energy—and whether you want it there or not.

Beyond your body, look at the energy around you. Does your energy flow out of you in places? Do you think it should? Why or why not? Or is there energy from outside of you that seems to be gnawing at your own energy? Give it a texture or color or words in your mind. If energy is seeping into your body, ask yourself if that's working for you or not. Keep in mind that not all energy from outside you is bad. What's most important is that you know what is affecting you and whether or not you want to keep it.

IN SUMMARY

Your energy—and especially your *understanding* of your energy—is going to be your most effective form of protection. This is not only about protection from ghosts and other entities; it's also about the protection your spirit naturally provides you when making day-to-day decisions in the physical world. The effort you put into understanding your body, mind, and soul will assist you in every area of your life.

HERE ARE SOME KEY POINTS TO REMEMBER:

- Understanding your own energy is your best form of protection.
- Soul energy examinations can be unique and multifaceted.
- Grounded mindfulness grows confidence.
- Mindful statements can make you feel like your own superhero.
- *Relaxed*, *cozy*, and *safe* can mean different things for different people.
- Body scans and energy examinations take practice; you'll get quicker at them as you gain experience.

CHAPTER 4

GETTING YOUR ENERGY READY FOR GHOST COMMUNICATION

One of the things people find scary about communicating with ghosts is the idea that the ghost will overpower them or take control of their energy. While it's true that ghosts can drain your energy or attach themselves to it, there are several ways you can prepare yourself to avoid these problems. In this chapter you'll learn all about the preparatory elements that go into keeping you safe when connecting with spirits. You'll find information on how to cleanse your energy, as well as tips for keeping your energy flow and balance clean throughout spiritual perception. You'll also learn how to best protect yourself through basic shielding practices that you'll build for yourself through fun, creative, and thought-provoking activities. You'll discover how proactive, mindful effort can make you feel more confident and prepared when getting ready to talk with ghosts. Lastly, I'll share some examples of what my personal shields look like for the various kinds of spiritual work that I do so that you have some ideas to start with when creating your own shields.

HOW TO BALANCE AND CLEANSE YOUR ENERGY

In order to balance and cleanse your energy, it's necessary to know where your personal energy begins and ends and—most importantly—how to get back to your fundamental base energy quickly. Your energy and how you perceive it consist of a variety of factors: your thoughts, your feelings, your emotions, and any other parts that make your life experience unique to you. By embracing those elements, you build a familiarity with your energy and the ability to call to it when needed. You also gain knowledge of what is *not* you or your energy so that you can quickly recognize outside energy and push it away from you when needed.

Finding Your Base Point

Knowing yourself and your personal energy is the first step to being able to properly perceive energy beyond yourself. The previous chapter was all about *you* understanding *you*. This chapter is about getting back to that center or base point quickly and at any time. Your base point is your starting point or first step to utilizing your psychic perception. You could also consider it a kind of base camp for yourself. What does it mean to go back to *you*? What is your starting point? To find this, you have to first understand yourself, without looking outward, either physically or psychically, to perceive what's around you. Your base point is not about anything else; it's only about returning to the first part of perception: understanding you.

Understanding yourself requires being present and mindful of how you're feeling. This can entail several things, including knowing how you're feeling physically, knowing how you're feeling emotionally, and knowing where your thoughts are and why. It's about connecting back with the soul energy part of the body scan we discussed in the previous chapter. Understanding that you are in control of yourself and that all these elements make up who you are—that is your base point.

Getting back to your base is important for many situations, but it's especially important when you're unsure of which energy is yours. You can get back to your base either by repeating the body scan methods from the previous chapter or by simply asking yourself, *Is this me? Am I feeling this? Why or why not?* For example, if you walk into a room and immediately feel sick to your stomach, it's important to ask yourself, *What's my base? What was I feeling five minutes ago?*

What changed? Sometimes the answer is clear: You walked into a new room. Sometimes you have to ask yourself harder questions, such as, *Why is everything making me angry all of a sudden? Is the anger mine? What is my base point?* Sometimes, refusing to claim the feelings that have affected you can be enough to make them go away. Other times, you may need to do a body scan and release any energy that is not yours. It's okay if you need to take a moment away from wherever you are to go back to your base point.

When you can understand where your energy started, you can understand what energy is yours and what energy you may be picking up on from your surroundings. Skipping this step can ultimately lead to confusion, skewed perception, and sometimes worse: confusion about yourself. Always check in with your energy first. Always know what your base point is.

What Does It Mean to Balance Your Energy?

Balancing your energy entails:

1. Understanding that there is an imbalance.
2. Doing something about it.

Once you know what your energy feels like, you can sense the imbalance that's created when anything that feels outside of your energy is let in. It is up to you to decide how much imbalance you want to take in before releasing it. Sometimes you can get a better understanding of the spiritual energy around you by allowing a temporary imbalance. For example, let's say a spirit had a knee injury when they were alive. As you approach the spirit—whether knowingly or unknowingly—you begin to have unexplained soreness in your knee. As you notice the change in your energy, you may want to feel out the soreness. You may want to ask yourself if it's a bone issue or a muscle one. If you have medical or anatomy knowledge, your answer may be more detailed. However, once you understand the issue, you no longer need to keep the energy in your body. The information was passed along to you, and you can now keep that new knowledge in mind without keeping the soreness in your knee.

A more nuanced example may be a sudden feeling of annoyance. Let's say you've had a go-go-go kind of evening. You're already tired when you finally arrive at the spot where you're looking to meet some ghosts. Perhaps in all the hustle you forgot to check in with your energy and get to your base point before beginning. You walk into a room. You're already on edge from the previous events. You feel even more on edge in that room, but you don't yet spot the amplified energy. Someone you're with accidentally bumps into you in the dark. You snap and yell at them to pay attention.

It's at this moment that you need to stop and ask yourself what your base point is. Sure, it's possible that you are just annoyed with the person you're with. However, if you aren't usually the type of person to lose your cool that quickly, you may need to ask yourself if there is an imbalance in your energy. Once your energy is balanced, perhaps you find that you're far less annoyed than you were minutes ago. You find you're able to pinpoint where the feeling of annoyance came from—and it was from outside of you.

Granted, it's important to take responsibility for your own behavior. Was the annoyance entirely yours? No. Did you snap and yell at someone, which was your own action? Yes. Remember: Your imbalance is not the ghost's fault. The ghost has enough to worry about. You read the energy correctly, but because your energy was not balanced, the ghost's energy was uncontrolled. It happens sometimes! Take note for your own learning and growth, and move on. In this example, moving on might include apologizing to the person you yelled at—and the apology might help balance your energy too.

Cleansing Your Energy

Cleansing your energy can start with an acknowledgment. Did something throw your energy out of balance? Acknowledge it, release it, and move on. It can really be that simple. Consider the techniques in Chapter 3 as routine maintenance. You may enjoy sitting in your own clean energy enough to do a full check-in every day. I certainly hope you do! However, when you're on the go, you'll find your process of getting back to base much faster once you know what to look for, and that's when the material in this chapter will come in handy.

Cleansing your energy is different from balancing your energy. Balance can work like a scale. Sometimes you allow your energy to become somewhat imbalanced in order to understand what it is you're perceiving. You return to balance by returning to your base point. To cleanse your energy is to wipe all external thoughts, feelings, emotions, sensations, and memories from your energy. You can continue to carry your personal memory of the experience you had, but it's not your responsibility to be carrying anyone else's memories around.

GHOSTLY GO-TO

Having a quick way to cleanse your energy is beneficial even when you're not dealing with ghosts. Have you ever been around someone who leaks negativity? Do you find yourself more weighed down and sluggish whenever you're around them? That is a sign of your imbalance. Acknowledge that the negative feeling is not yours, and let it go.

Ways to Cleanse Energy

The previous chapter taught the basics of an energy cleanse through the body scan technique. Now, you will learn how to add some extra elements to that base to make a cleansing routine that is all yours. You may want to cleanse at the beginning of the day to get your thoughts straight, after leaving a particularly offensive ghost, or at the end of a stressful work day. Make your routines fun, empowering, and magical so you will feel good about using them with regularity.

It's important to note that the materials you use to cleanse your energy are like the oil that keeps gears running smoothly. You are the machine. Your words and your beliefs are the most important factors for a successful cleanse. Anything that helps you feel safe and provides you a sense of balance can be considered a cleanse. As you're building your practice I recommend mixing and matching different kinds of cleansing so that your process is all yours. Here are some examples:

- **Smoke Cleanse:** Light herbs, herb bundles, specific kinds of woods, and/or incense on fire to create smoke. As the smoke moves around, imagine that it repels energy that doesn't balance with you. You may wave it over your head, arms, back, chest, and legs. Be sure you're in a ventilated location so that the smoke has somewhere to release to.

GHOSTLY GO-TO

Smudging with white sage has become synonymous with smoke cleanses; however, that is a vastly incorrect translation of the practice. Smudging with white sage is a closed practice sacred to First Americans. Smoke cleansing, depending on what type of substance is being used, is an open practice used by many across the world.

- **Simmer Pot Cleanse:** Combine various herbs, fruits, and spices, and place them in a pot to boil. As the aroma rises, allow your sense of smell to settle with it. Let the steam and smell surround you by waving it over your head, arms, chest, and legs. Ask the elements to help cleanse your energy and bring it back to balance.
- **Water Cleanse:** Blessed water can come in various forms. It may be from a simmer pot you made. It may be from your favorite river under a particular moon cycle that made you feel good. It may be intentionally blessed by a spiritual practitioner just

as holy water is blessed by a priest. Be sure whatever water you use is safe to have on your skin. You may place it on different points, such as on your forehead, shoulders, heart, hands, knees, and feet. Or you may decide to use the water to draw lines on your body. You may also take an intentional shower or bath. Depending on the paint or texture of your walls, you may decide to draw symbols or sigils of safety using the water.

- **Food/Tea Cleanse:** Ingesting food or drink can be a form of cleansing. A specific kind of tea may bring you peace. Or you may eat a certain food, placing an intention within it that helps to remove any sticky energy from your body. Different teas and foods may have different meanings for each person, and that's okay. I simply recommend using foods that are natural and as minimally processed as possible.
- **Sound Cleanse:** Traditional sound cleanses might use singing bowls, bells, chimes, or drums. While these ways are still very effective, in modern times, we have even more ways to sound cleanse. And yes, if music that inspires head banging is a cleanse to you, you can absolutely use that. You may also want to use binaural beats that are specific to anti-anxiety and cleansing. Listening to a recording that leads you through a meditation may also be considered a sound cleanse. Whatever you utilize, let the sound seep into your energy with the intention that it can remove anything you want to get rid of.

- **Dance Cleanse:** This is where the head-banging sound cleanse can be effective. Dancing is a timeless way of connecting with your energy. Whether it's stomping hard enough to feel the beat in your bones, jumping around, or even moving in choreographed and performative ways, all dancing is a great way to reconnect to your mind, body, and soul.

The act of cleansing your energy before communicating with ghosts is a critical step in protecting yourself. Once you've cleansed your energy, you are ready to move on to the next step, which is building and putting on your shield.

GHOSTLY GO-TO

Materials and tools to cleanse your energy can include (in no particular order) blue or green sage, rosemary, pine, cedar, eucalyptus, orange, cranberry, apple, cinnamon, rose, lavender, singing bowls, bells, herbal teas, kale, spinach, and Brussels sprouts.

HOW TO SHIELD

Shielding begins and ends with the cognitive decision that your energy—physically, mentally, and emotionally—is worth protecting. A shield acts as a boundary to remind you and anything else that may be in the room with you that your energy is yours alone. You'll find that building a shield can be less about keeping distance and more about claiming your own energetic space.

What Is a Shield?

A shield is any way you protect your state of energetic balance. It is a spiritual manifestation of the mental protections and boundaries you keep for yourself. I've heard some people say they want to be open to *anything* in the spiritual world. But I always ask them, "Would you be open to any physical person in the same way? To let them tell you what to think? How to feel? Where to go?" Without fail, their answer is always no. Ghosts once inhabited physical forms. Treat them the same way as you would treat the living. Have the same reservations.

The good news is, if you can keep up boundaries with physical people, you can easily apply that skill to creating an energetic shield. Some people subconsciously create shields based on their life experience. When I meet someone and think, *They're so guarded*, I consider that either consciously or subconsciously, that person is energetically shielded.

GHOSTLY GO-TO

Energetic shields can take a variety of different forms. Some people like to anchor their shields in objects that they wear. My hesitation related to this practice is that you want to be sure you can still use the shield you create in the event the object is lost or forgotten. Sometimes objects may disappear because they have taken an energetic hit in order to protect you. For example, I once used an obsidian stone on a necklace for part of my protection. One day I woke up, went over to where I had left it, and the stone had vanished from where it had been on the necklace the night before. While I'm not sure what I needed to be protected from, I trusted that whatever happened needed to happen. This experience led me to getting a new piece of protective jewelry within the week.

I encourage you to create a shield using your ability to pull energy in from the infinite around you, rather than using the finite energy within your own physical form. The energy should never come from you; rather, it should be pulled either up or down. (I will go into specifics on this in the later section on how to put on your shield.) Once in place, your shield should not be heavy or a burden; it should just be there. As long as your intention is clear and strong, you can trust your shield to work. Your making the decision that your shield works is the magic of the shield.

Why Should You Shield?

While most spirits are not malicious, many of them do not understand what energy they can draw from. As an example from the living, have you ever known someone who needs constant validation and encouragement? They may be the kindest person you've ever known, but they constantly stop you and ask you to go out of your way to offer them validation. This is someone who requires the energy of others to function because they do not understand how to create balance within themselves. Ghosts can be very similar.

Imagine being stuck for a hundred years or so. You get caught up in immobility and begin to accept your fate. You may forget who you are or why you're even there. Suddenly, a person arrives. They seem to glow. They ask you about yourself. They want your name. They seem to care about you—when you'd forgotten you could care about *anything*, let alone yourself. You may reach out to them. You may want them to ask you more and to help you remember. You begin to hang onto them for gratification rather than looking inward to your own energy. This situation can quickly become exhausting for everyone involved.

Shielding is a reminder—to yourself, as well as to anything around you—that your energy is your own. You can certainly work with a spirit to help them find themself, but they should not need to lean on your energy to do that. They need to learn to balance themself. It's even possible that you can teach them the skills you learn here.

Shielding is also important because not all spirits have good intentions. Some of them are as disgusting in death as they were in life. I've been to places where the ghosts of horrific murderers were found. For example, an alleged

Jack the Ripper found my existence insulting and began to project images and physical feelings of just what he wanted to do to me. I started to get gut and head pains from his thoughts. In the moment, I merely reminded myself that the feeling represented an imbalance. I understood its implication, did a quick cleanse to get back to my base point, checked that my shield was in place well enough to keep his hideous projections out of my mind and body, and went about the investigation.

GHOSTLY GO-TO

The idea of protecting your mental space is backed by psychology. Practicing self-awareness, curating the information you consume, and surrounding yourself with people you align with are recommended as ways to protect your mental world.

The shield you use to protect your psychic world can look any way you want it to. It can *do* anything you want it to. It can close you off from spiritual activity just as well as it can open you up to it. I often get asked if experiencing spirits is exhausting and if I see ghosts all the time. Absolutely not! If I were seeing spirits all the time, how would I ever have peace and quiet? Psychic perception is meant to amplify your life, not control it. That is why shielding is a must.

How to Build Your Shield

When building your shield, I encourage you to be inspired by what is already close to you. For example:

- Do you like elements of nature? Then think, *How does a tree protect itself?*
- Are you a fantasy genre enthusiast? Explore what protections your favorite characters have.
- Perhaps you're into action movies and comic book characters. What sorts of elements do they have to protect them?
- Maybe you are inspired by animals. What can an animal teach you about protection?
- If you love history, find a suit of armor that you believe is most effective.
- Like science fiction? Try using the Force.

Some people may be able to quiet their spiritual experiences by visualizing that they are turning off a switch. Or perhaps your shield looks like a concrete bunker or a solid brick wall. Maybe you want the bunker to have a high-strength window so that you're not entirely cut off from awareness. Some people may want to be fully aware but untouched. You can always surround yourself with bulletproof glass so that you get the full picture.

Be as specific as possible about your shield. Draw it out, or find photos. Make this a creative project. Be sure you understand what each element does to protect you. It may help you to write out a description of your shield as if you were writing a story. If you know someone else who's growing their spiritual awareness, you may like to go over your shield with them and ask for their feedback.

Change your shield as needed for the environment you find yourself in. Always know you can go back to your balanced base point as needed. Whether with ghosts or people, remember that you can always excuse yourself to reconnect with yourself and your energy. Release what you need to, and build your shield back up to fit your situation.

PUTTING ON YOUR SHIELD

Your daily habit of choosing and putting on clothes prepares you for the rest of your day. Shielding is no different. You most likely don't remember when you learned the steps of putting on your clothes; it has simply evolved into an automatic practice requiring little thought on your part. Shielding is the same. Once you know how to put your unique shield on and have it work, the process won't take you more than a few seconds. However, you must first understand how to get to that comfortable place. The following steps will help you build and put on your shield.

Step One: Envision Your Shield

Envisioning your shield may mean seeing it in your head as a picture you created. It could also mean speaking the elements of your shield (either out loud or in your head). Or you could envision it by touching an element or texture that reminds you of your shield. Perhaps you will need to utilize all these steps. You may not always need to do several steps to envision your shield, but when you're starting out it's good to have on hand anything that helps you.

Step Two: Put On Your Shield

While you can put on your shield just in your mind, I personally like to add the element of physical play. If your shield looks like a suit of armor, what actions would you do to put that on? If your shield is fire, what strikes the flame, and how does it cover your body safely? Whatever you choose, remember the process of putting on the suit in Marvel's Iron Man movies. At first, it was complex and took time and effort. Over time, a button on a wristwatch did the trick and the suit knew where to go and what to do on its own.

GHOSTLY GO-TO

Be sure that the energy of your shield isn't coming from your core, as this can lead to exhaustion. Pull your shield either down from the sky like rain or up from the ground like a plant. Take inspiration from the simplicity of nature.

Step Three: Speak It Into Existence

While most of the time you can speak your shield into existence in your mind, at some point you should try saying the words out loud so that your ears can hear them. The words you say can change according to what you need. The point is that you believe the words you say. I often say something like, *This is my impenetrable shield. Nothing is allowed through without my consent.* You may choose to say something like, *Only that which means me well may be perceived while my shield is on*. Make it unique to you. Whatever you choose to say, make sure it elicits a feeling of personal empowerment to seal its power and connection to you.

Step Four: Maintenance

Just as a physical shield may require maintenance, so may your energetic shield. The important point is that you catch any problems and repair them. If someone else's emotions are leaking in, understand that they are not your own, then check your shield. If you feel too imbalanced throughout an experience, you may need to go back and check the elements of your shield in addition to your self-belief.

GHOSTLY GO-TO

As a habit, every time I use the bathroom I clean my energy and check my shield. I've made this part of my everyday routine. As I use the bathroom and wash my hands, I cleanse. Before I leave the bathroom, I say my shield words and envision my shield. It can really be that simple.

Step Five: Release

You never have to take off your shield. However, if there are places where you feel safe and people you feel safe with, you can relax your shield and allow your energy to blend. I tend to relax my shield in my bedroom and when I'm with my closest friends and family. That's because I know that place and those people to be safe. If your shield being on all the time feels the safest to you, that is fine too.

GHOSTLY GO-TO

According to some psychological studies, imagination is the key to making long-term change to one's life. Being able to inwardly see, feel, and experience something that you created to make yourself safe is a step toward manifesting real safety outside of you as well.

SHIELD EXAMPLES AND PURPOSES

The following is a list of shields I've used over the years. I hope that these examples will help you create your own shield. Feel free to use these and combine or recreate them as you like!

Lantern

WHAT IT LOOKS LIKE: A light that shines all around me—I am the lantern.

WHAT IT DOES: It allows me to see truth. The beam creates an energetic frequency that doesn't allow anything to come in. Sometimes I electrify the light for extra effect. It doesn't hurt anyone as long as they respectfully keep their distance.

Drenching Winds

WHAT IT LOOKS LIKE: Similar to a tornado, but with raindrops that fly so fast they sting.

WHAT IT DOES: It makes me look a lot less approachable, and that's the point! I can't always see out of this shield, and spirits definitely don't get to see in.

Dr. Strange-Inspired Shield

WHAT IT LOOKS LIKE: A transparent shield with glowing, shimmery gold markings that hold it together.

WHAT IT DOES: It makes me look magical, which is not always of interest to ghosts. I use this shield a lot with the living in order to take up space and not get stepped on.

Obsidian Shards

WHAT IT LOOKS LIKE: A small, moving mountain of black obsidian points.

WHAT IT DOES: If anything touches me, it will be pricked. If anyone runs at me, they will get hurt. It's a shield that says, *Do not mess with me*. I use this in dangerous places.

Two-Way Mirror

WHAT IT LOOKS LIKE: A mirror that's shaped like an egg around me. It shows people themselves rather than revealing the details of my presence.

WHAT IT DOES: It refocuses attention back on the viewer and only allows them to see me if I utilize a lantern effect from inside. This is a multilayer shield.

GHOST STORY

BATTLESHIP *NORTH CAROLINA*

The intention of an effective shield will inherently dictate the experience you have in a haunted location. The more specificity behind what a shield does, the less likely you are to run into a frightening or even uncomfortable situation with a ghost. This was the lesson my friend and I learned when visiting one of my state's most famously haunted ships.

The USS *North Carolina* is not only one of the hottest tourist spots in the state—it's also one of the most haunted. I've found this location to be perfect for anyone looking to grow their abilities in perceiving spirits. This vast ship was used during the Second World War. While many spirits linger there, very few are of people who passed away while on the vessel. The location is more of a hangout for veteran ghosts of all ages looking to relive their days in the navy.

A caveat to consider here is that by the time I visited the battleship *North Carolina*, I had already developed some shielding techniques. I knew the place to be haunted, and I knew to keep my wits about me. I couldn't say the same for the friend I brought with me. While this friend was well into her spiritual journey, she was new to understanding that shielding was an option. Up until that point she had simply been affected, and sometimes exhausted, by the spiritual activity that was around her.

There are two considerations here:

1. My shielding was a lot stronger than it needed to be, as I was tired from a restless night that was unrelated to the present events.
2. Due to a similarly restless night being in a highly haunted city she wasn't accustomed to, her shielding was not as strong as it could have been.

That combination led to my friend being overwhelmed by ghosts—and to me hardly feeling anything.

As my friend and I descended the stairs and made our way into the depths of the ship, I stopped short when I heard my friend gasp. I looked back. Tears were in her eyes. Her hand was over her chest. All she seemed to know was that a young man was hurting. The emotions of his pain were overwhelming her. As I lessened my own barriers, I could see a young man no more than twenty years old standing nearby.

Both my friend and the ghost were making the same strained, horrified expression. I felt the root of the ghost's fear: He worried he would never make it home. My friend's empathy seemed to enhance the ghost's feelings. He wanted to cry. She was wiping away tears. He wanted to leave. She wanted to leave. Both stood as if stuck—in two very different times and yet in the same place.

The poor man's energy pleaded for help. He didn't want to be there, stuck in the mind he was in. I asked my friend to reground her energy so that she would be connected with herself rather than with this man. She did what she could, but I could tell it was difficult, as their energy was blending. I asked the man what home looked like. Through my mind's eye I began to see what he saw. A simple white house with green shutters. A woman who may have been his wife or sister. A feeling of warm supper having just been laid out. I pulled some energy up, gave it to him, told him to think of home, and sent him on his way. (I did not move the man on; I asked him what *he* wanted and then I supplied him with the energy to get there. I merely provided him with the energetic "gas" he needed to drive to that part of himself that he associated as home.)

The feeling of sadness and terror was gone. My friend began to breathe steadily again. Her tears left. She felt

sympathy for the man, but she was no longer overwhelmed by it. I reminded her to shield so that the experiences wouldn't feel as intense. We moved forward and continued to meet spirits, and everyone else we met that day was doing just fine.

IN SUMMARY

The intensity of spiritual experiences comes down to the energy of the person looking to experience them. Just as shields can protect your energy from prying ghosts, they can also keep you from connecting with anything at all. Being able to grow your psychic mediumship abilities comes down to understanding the limits of your own energetic balance, followed by taking control of protecting your energy as needed to avoid getting overwhelmed.

HERE ARE SOME KEY POINTS TO REMEMBER:

- You can return to your base point (a point where you exist with only *your* energy) at any time you choose.
- Temporarily imbalanced energy can assist you with understanding psychic information, but you should always rebalance your energy after you've gained the understanding you need.
- There are many different ways to cleanse. What's most important is that you find a way that works for you.
- Shielding is a must if you want to keep your energetic balance safe.
- Building a shield should be a fun, creative, and empowering activity.

CHAPTER 5

UNDERSTANDING HOW TO SENSE SPIRITS

Have you ever walked into a new place and somehow "known" something about its past? Have you ever caught a strange scent that didn't match your surroundings? Have you ever seen a shadow move out of the corner of your eye or heard a voice in the air? If so, you were most likely experiencing something through one of your psychic senses. This chapter will break down the multiple senses involved in psychic perception. You will learn what each sense is and see examples of how each one can manifest for you and stories of how I personally have experienced and grown each skill. You'll also learn about fun activities that you can do to boost your psychic development.

DISCOVERING PSYCHIC SENSES

Unfortunately there is not enough discussion of what psychic senses are and how they appear in everyday life. Less than a decade ago, I had never heard anyone discuss in any kind of detail how a person could come to understand they were psychic. From what I could gather, a person was either super psychic and could see, hear, and sense the entire spiritual plane, or they were entirely blind to it all. Because of this, when I started having my own experiences with ghosts, I did not consider myself psychic or a medium. Like me, many people are having spiritual interactions they aren't even aware of—or even spiritual interactions that they notice but dismiss—because they don't understand how psychic skills actually work. This is just what happened to me until a psychic friend validated my experience.

GHOST STORY

AM I PSYCHIC?

Back in October 2020, I regularly found myself casually talking with a spirit that I met outside of the Burgwin-Wright House in Wilmington, North Carolina. However, as far as I knew, I could have very well been making him up. The first night that I met this ghost, I went back to my roommate and told him that I may have just met a ghost from the American Revolution, but I wasn't really sure if that had happened or not. My roommate basically said, "That's cool," and we didn't say anything else about it. After all, we had both been living in a highly haunted area ever since we moved to Wilmington. Meeting ghosts was a thing that sometimes just sort of happened.

Almost every night that I found myself working downtown, I would walk by the house. This British soldier wearing a full uniform and red coat was consistently waiting for me in the same spot each night. He would always offer to walk me home, because it made him uncomfortable to see me, a single woman, walking alone at night. Sometimes I would let him follow about halfway before telling him to leave me. I didn't want to give away information on where I lived. After a while, though, I started to sense that he meant me no harm, and I let him walk me the whole way home.

I remember that, when I looked at him, I saw something like an overlay—a combination of what my mind wanted me to see before me, and what was actually there. I had trouble believing that I was clairvoyant enough to see a ghost. I remember seeing his features. I remember hearing his voice, but it seemed to come from just inside my ear. I remember feeling how gentle he was whenever he spoke to me. I could also sense in him a kind of confusion; it's an emotion that, since this encounter, I've often seen in ghosts who are not entirely sure where they are anymore. I had all of this detailed information, but I was still unsure if I was somehow making it all up.

Life led me away from Wilmington for about a five-month period. When I came back to Wilmington, I returned to the same spot where I'd visited this ghost before. It was strange. Part of me felt like he should be there, but I couldn't see him in my mind the way I had before. The gentleness that I had associated him with had turned into a kind of coldness that I didn't understand. I began to surmise that this coldness might mean that the ghost was angry with me for my absence. I went to the spot more than once and, not seeing him, I began to wonder if I had been talking to no one. It made me feel defeated and unsure of anything that I had previously experienced.

I was fortunate to have a spiritually sensitive friend visiting town. I offered to show him and his wife around to some of my favorite spots downtown. I felt validated as we walked around and he experienced a lot of sensations similar to what I had felt. I was very nervous when we approached the Burgwin-Wright House. I hoped that, after he'd validated so many of my other experiences throughout the evening, my friend would also be able to tell me if I had actually been picking up on a ghost in that location or not.

As I stood near the spot where the ghost had always offered to walk me home, I once again felt the sensations that I had been experiencing in that place since my return to Wilmington. I saw my friend's eyes move slowly behind me and up and up toward the height of someone else. My friend made a funny face and then relaxed. He asked who my friend was. I asked him who he meant.

My friend said, "The soldier standing behind you. Who is he?"

I asked him what color the man's coat was.

My friend said, without a pause, "Red."

For a short time, my friend and I went back and forth about what else we picked up on regarding the man behind me. I was so relieved I wanted to cry. My friend had had no idea about this ghost before I introduced them to each other. We came up with the same description and the same answers. It was then that I could acknowledge that, just as the living may change, so may those who have passed over. The ghost I had befriended seemed to have grown. I had once understood him to feel lost and a little desperate, but now, some months later, he seemed more steady and resolute in his presence. His newfound groundedness had thrown me at first and made me doubt myself. It was through that experience that I finally gained the confidence to believe that my abilities were more than just my imagination.

USING YOUR PSYCHIC SENSES

Just as you have five senses of physical perception, you also have seven psychic or spiritual senses of perception. These senses are often rolled into one idea called the sixth sense. These psychic senses advance and mirror your physical senses. Understand that just as your physical senses are not isolated to singular forms of perception, your psychic senses also do not function on an isolated basis, but if you understand how each sense functions on its own, you can also understand how these senses work with one another to create a well-rounded experience when meeting a ghost.

The seven psychic senses are:

- Claircognizance
- Clairvoyance
- Clairaudience
- Clairtangency
- Clairemotion/Clairsentience
- Clairsalience
- Clairgustance

The following sections will explain what each of these senses is and how the psychic senses can alert you to spirits. I would encourage you to utilize the activities and to treat your psychic sense development like a game. That way, your brain will associate utilizing your psychic skill set with fun and safety. Take your time as needed. The point here is just for you to understand that you can use different senses when perceiving and talking to ghosts.

GHOSTLY GO-TO

In 2009 a Pew Research Center survey revealed that 18 percent of American adults believed they had witnessed a ghost. By 2025, a Gallup poll reported as many as 39 percent believed in ghosts.

Claircognizance: "I Know . . ."

WHAT IT IS: Claircognizance is, in essence, your intuition. When something pops into your mind—new information and not something you could have concluded in a straightforward manner based on your surroundings and knowledge—that is claircognizance. Someone with a strong and confident sense of claircognizance can use this skill to fill in blanks their other senses may have trouble perceiving.

HOW TO USE IT: If you couldn't see, hear, smell, taste, touch, or emotively feel, ask yourself, *What would you know?* Let a thought come from seemingly out of nowhere. This is not a conclusion that results from a train of thought. This is a seemingly random thought that just pops in. To use claircognizance to strengthen another psychic sense, clear your mind and ask yourself, *What do I know I see, hear, smell, or feel?*

Examples:

- Entering a new place and "knowing" something happened there.
- Seeing a modern object and knowing something else used to be in the same place.
- "Knowing" you're not alone.

ACTIVITY: Without looking up any of its history, go to a location that you're not familiar with. This may be best to do with a friend who can take you somewhere that you've never been. I encourage you to go to a historic place so that you can later check your information with staff or informative signs. You may want to keep your eyes down when you're getting close to the location. Once you've arrived, ask yourself, *What do I know happened here?* Set a timer and write everything you can for at least five minutes. Writing down your reads can be especially beneficial because you may say or think things and then forget them later. Set yourself up for success from the beginning! You can also speak out everything you think. Once you can't seem to know anymore, go exploring to see what validations you can find.

KEEP IN MIND: The killer of self-trust and claircognizance is anxiety! The energy of anxiety sits just outside the head. It is not connected to the present energy of the now. If anxious thoughts are filling your mind, go back to the mindfulness section in Chapter 3 and check your balance. Claircognizance is clear connection, not cluttered deflection.

Clairvoyance: "I See . . ."

WHAT IT IS: *Clairvoyance* has become a catchall for psychic ability. Specifically, it is the ability to *see* spiritual or psychic information. It can work two ways:

- **Physical-eye clairvoyance** is being able to see spiritual energy with your eyes. This may include, but is not limited to, seeing shadow figures, balls of light or orbs, figures with details, waves of energy, auras, and so on.
- **Inner-eye clairvoyance** is more common. This is the ability to utilize the images of the mind's eye rather than the perceptions of the physical eye alone. Visions may come through as far- or nearsighted, and you should use your mind to focus in or zoom out accordingly to create the clearest possible picture with your mind.

HOW TO USE IT: You may sometimes see a spirit with your eyes—and then see it fade. This is often a result of focusing too hard with your eyes to check whether or not the image you saw was physically there. Our eyes have been formed through evolution to spot details. Clairvoyance works the opposite way: You often have to have your eyes *out* of focus in order to see. If you saw a figure and lost it, close your eyes and replay what happened in your mind's eye. Freeze the image in your mind and zoom in or zoom out. Get as detailed as possible. Don't be surprised if you find yourself beginning to see where the spirit is in real time rather than just where you remember it being. If you don't see anything physically to begin with, try starting with your eyes closed or unfocused and asking your mind to paint a clearer picture for you.

Examples:

- Seeing spots in graveyards or in historic or known haunted areas.
- Seeing things out of the corner of your eye in specific places.
- A vast imagination that paints images that tell you more about a location than you could have otherwise known.

ACTIVITY: Go to a place that you understand to be haunted. Make sure it's a place you feel comfortable in. Your safety is very important. If you go in expecting to be scared, you will be scared. So, for this exercise, go into a place that feels comfortable to you. Bring along something you can write with. Once you get there, relax your vision. Scan the area. Does anything seem more out of focus than everything else? Do you pick up on any wavy energy? Do you pick up on any unexplained darkness? It may help you to draw, for yourself, a map of where you are. Move toward the places where you felt the most clarity from your initial read. You may either draw or write out bullet points of any descriptive features that you get from those points. If all you are seeing is a single color, ask yourself, *What does that color mean to me?* If you're seeing specific attributes of a person, such as a hairstyle or a kind of shoe, make a note of those and zoom out as needed to get a full picture. Or you may need to do the opposite: If you feel like you're seeing everything at once, zoom in to get details. Start from either the top of the head or the bottom of the feet, and work your way through what you're seeing. Get as descriptive as you can. Act as if you were an author explaining to readers exactly what you see. Then do some exploring! Look up any history you can on the location. Look up ghost stories. You may not always get immediate confirmation of your reads, but that is not the point. The point is that your mind was not sculpting in an image for you; rather, it was provided an image from outside of your consciousness.

KEEP IN MIND: If you're seeing spots or waves of energy all the time, definitely get your eyes checked medically to make sure there isn't an underlying physical issue. However, if these experiences only happen in specific places, that can indicate a haunting or other spiritual activity. If you are constantly seeing bugs out of the corner of your eyes, this may also be a sign of a medical or psychological condition. It's nothing to be afraid of; just be sure you get the information you need to accurately assess what's happening.

Clairaudience: "I Hear . . ."

WHAT IT IS: Clairaudience is the ability to hear spiritual activity such as voices, music, sounds of the past, and so on. While most people may not know they have this skill, many have inner-ear clairaudience and do not realize it. There are two types of clairaudience:

- ***Physical-Ear Clairaudience:*** People most commonly hear spiritual activity right before they fall asleep. Many report hearing their name or muffled conversations. This is no coincidence! Right as you're about to sleep, your brain enters theta state, and that's the same state used for channeling. It's also no coincidence that as soon as you wake up and look for the source of the voices, they're no longer there. The more focused your brain is on your survival state in the physical world, the less relaxed it will be to pick up on the spiritual. There must be balance.
- ***Inner-Ear Clairaudience:*** I find it easiest to describe this as when you either *feel* a spirit said something or *know* something was just said. This may feel like an inner dialogue with another in your head. Depending on how apt you are, some words may come through a little fuzzy, especially if your mind isn't familiar with them. These may be words that aren't in your vocabulary or words that come from a different language entirely. However, by supplementing clairaudience with claircognizance, you will likely be able to fill in the gaps.

GHOSTLY GO-TO

The theta state is a naturally occurring pattern of brain waves where the brain relaxes into a daydreamy or half-awake, half-asleep state. This is the state where the brain is most able to meditate to receive intuitive information for spiritual connection, art, creative ventures, and emotional healing.

HOW TO USE IT: Your brain has a natural proclivity for keeping you sane. What a relief! So, when you hear a voice from the spirit world, the message often seems like it comes through as your own voice. To better distinguish your own mind's narrative from other voices, note whether or not the words use first person (*I*/*me*) or third person (*you*). Note what kinds of words are used and how they're used. Do you speak that way? If not, check into what or who you're hearing.

Examples:

- Internal conversations in your mind.
- Ear-ringing or pressure—either in haunted places or when you need to pay attention.
- Hearing someone or something that's seemingly not there.

ACTIVITY: Any enhancement you can do to hone the physical sense of hearing, you can also apply to clairaudience. This may mean going to a crowded place and focusing on individual voices, or going to an orchestra performance and concentrating on the sounds of specific instruments. As you do this, say to yourself, *I am acknowledging my physical hearing in order to strengthen my psychic hearing.* Should you have experiences where you hear voices, remind yourself that the voices are not dangerous. They are simply voices. The longer you can stay in a relaxed state, the more you will be able to hear, and in more detail. You may even be able to telepathically reach out to the voices you are hearing to ask them questions. Hearing things that are seemingly not there can be very jarring. The trick is to tell your brain that you are in control and that you are safe. Then you can open up and hear further.

KEEP IN MIND: If you're hearing voices everywhere you go and they're telling you negative information and/or to harm yourself and/or other people, please see a mental health professional. Psychic abilities can be shielded and blocked. Voices that are unwelcome and uncontrollable are a mental health issue that must be worked through with a professional. Similarly, some auditory experiences stem from physical health issues. If you are constantly hearing buzzing or have pressure that feels like you're under water, please see a doctor. In either of these cases, you deserve relief!

Clairtangency or Psychometry: "I Physically Feel . . ."

WHAT IT IS: Clairtangency is physically feeling sensations that cannot be detected or explained by the ordinary senses. Sometimes it is subtle and easy to brush away; in other cases it can be overwhelming and feel very real. Some who are clairtangent may feel a chill, whereas others may feel the impression of a hand on their own. It is also possible for a ghost to have enough energy to directly affect a person with great specificity. Experiences differ from person to person and place to place depending on the strength and understanding of the connection.

HOW TO USE IT: Some people have the same sensation whenever they pick up on spiritual activity. As you strengthen your awareness, you will learn to detect differences between different physical feelings. Some people feel sick when they need to leave. Some people feel warm when they ought to stay. The only way to know how you perceive is to acknowledge your ability and try it out in places where you feel safe. I like to use my clairtangency like a sonar reader. I send out little waves around me to pick up on energy shifts in electromagnetic energy nearby. You can even practice this with the living. If you were ever good at the intuitive game Four Corners as a kid, you were likely using clairtangency.

Examples:

- Temperature changes: suddenly feeling hot or cold in specific spots in a room or in specific parts of your body.
- Coughing or light choking (for example, experienced at the site of a hanging).
- Feeling like there's little room to move—even when your other senses tell you there's plenty of space around you.
- Physically feeling someone enter the room due to the electromagnetic shift the energy of the spirit brings.

ACTIVITY: I recommend playing this game with a trusted spirit you know. This may mean a passed loved one who you feel is around. It may mean a spirit guide. It may mean a deity who you trust. Sometimes the easiest spirits to feel are those that are closest to our physical plane: ghosts and passed loved ones. But who you will be able to feel really depends on where your natural frequency sits. If you don't feel a spirit on a particular frequency, I recommend trying a different frequency. To avoid confusion, be sure that you only try this activity with one being at a time. Ask the spirit to touch you in a consensual place. This may be your shoulder, a specific part of your arm, or a similar place that's comfortable for you. Note any physical differences that come about once you have asked them to touch you. Then ask them to pull away. Note any changes in sensation. Repeat this process, allowing yourself to notice any differences that you feel. As you grow more confident in this, let the spirit lead the game. Rather than asking them to place a hand on you and take it off, ask them to choose their own timing. You can also replicate this activity with physical people. Close your eyes and ask someone you trust to put a hand out very close to your body without touching it. Without overthinking it, say where you think their hand is. Then open your eyes. If you're having trouble, simply remind yourself that this is a natural ability that has been handed to us through millions of years of evolution. Always maintain your connection to the physical plane first; this will ground you to our plane and keep you in control of your senses.

KEEP IN MIND: Nothing should be allowed to physically harm you. If you are seeing scratches or feel like you can't breathe, make sure to cleanse, shield, and leave the location immediately! You should never put yourself into an abusive situation for the sake of psychic connection. Nothing that means you well will willingly hurt you.

Clairemotion/Clairsentience: "I Emotionally Feel . . ."

WHAT IT IS: Clairemotion is the ability to feel a spirit's emotion, either through experiencing it within oneself or through knowing what emotion is in a room. This type of psychic feeling specifically has to do with your emotions and how you feel on the inside. This is a skill set that those who think of themselves as empaths will thrive at. Many people say that being an empath is a learned trait that develops based upon how you are raised. Regardless of how you became an empath, you can grow the ability to sense spirits' emotions, just as you can learn the ability to do the same with physical people.

HOW TO USE IT: When walking into a new place or when you think you are connecting with a spirit, ask yourself, *If this experience were an emotion, what emotion would it be?* If you're having trouble figuring out what emotion you're feeling, I highly recommend consulting an emotion wheel. Emotion wheels can be found online; they help people better understand their emotions by naming and visually organizing specific feelings. The emotional state of a spirit in the room may cause you to experience the same emotion. Remember: It's okay to be temporarily thrown off balance by an outside emotion. Just be sure to notice the information that you're receiving and release it as needed so that you can maintain your own base point.

Examples:

- When you feel a new emotion even though nothing in your environment has changed and no specific line of thought has led you to the feeling.
- When you feel an emotion and have no idea where it came from—for example, wanting to cry or laugh for no apparent reason.
- Feeling suddenly very uncomfortable with no indication as to why.

ACTIVITY: Practice using this sense with the living first. Have a friend sit near you. Make sure that you can't see them, and ask them to be as quiet as possible. Have them scroll through social media and watch whatever comes across their screen in its entirety. Before they scroll on have them really *feel* what it is they're watching. Sometimes this is easiest to do if they watch a wide variety of content—for example, some news or political commentary, followed by a couple of funny videos. As they watch a video, write down what you think they're feeling. Before they scroll on to the next video, have them also write down what they were feeling. You can compare your answers either after each video or after five to ten different videos. I encourage you to do this activity with somebody who knows their emotions very well and is very open to talking about them. To try this with spirits, write down ten to fifteen questions that could cause an emotional response. The goal is not to traumatize anybody; rather, it is to ask questions that inspire visceral feelings in whoever you're talking to. One I commonly use is *Do you like tuna sandwiches?* People seem to either love or hate tuna, and there's little in between—enjoyment and disgust are two very different feelings. You can do this activity with just about any spirit that you trust. This can be a great way to get to know the spirits around you in a fun and relaxed way!

KEEP IN MIND: Being able to pick up on someone else's emotions does not require you to absorb the emotions within your own energy! This is often an assumption and mistake that people make when they refer to themselves as empaths. You can understand how someone is feeling without letting it affect your own energy. If you are concerned that you are absorbing too much energy that is not your own, whether it's from a present spiritual experience or from experiences from your past, make sure to check yourself. Do what you need to do to return yourself back to balance. Review the mindfulness section in Chapter 3 and get any necessary mental health help you may need. You want to be sure you're reading the feelings in your present, not those of your or someone else's past.

GHOSTLY GO-TO

Synesthesia is a neurological condition where an experience with one sense causes connected sensations in another sense. There are different kinds. Some people see colors when feeling different emotional states or hearing different sounds. Some people can taste words.

Clairsalience: "I Smell . . ."

WHAT IT IS: Clairsalience is being able to smell something that is not physically there. This is a common psychic skill that most people possess; people often brush clairsalient experiences away, assuming they are ordinary physical perceptions. Clairsalient perceptions can be excellent indicators that it's time to tune into other forms of psychic perception. Sometimes it can be very hard to understand why you're smelling something that you have no way to explain. Clairsalience can also be fueled by claircognizance. Sometimes you just know that a place should smell a certain way, even though you can't physically smell it. You might call that experience a kind of inner-nose clairsalience.

HOW TO USE IT: If you have natural clairsalience, it can be very easy to use! Sometimes smells can become very uncomfortable. If this should happen, take the information you need, and then be sure to set your energy back to balance.

Examples:

- Smelling death, disease, or excrement in an otherwise clean environment.
- Smelling cigarette smoke or perfume when no one else is around.
- Smelling a barn or machinery in a repurposed building.

ACTIVITY: To strengthen this ability, you can smell different perfumes and try to deconstruct the ingredients. As you do this, remind yourself that you are using your physical sense of smell in order to strengthen your psychic sense of smell. You can also sharpen your sense of smell by spending time in a big city where there are a lot of different kinds of smells all in one area. To turn this sense toward the spirit world, visit a historic city, such as Savannah, Georgia, that has been well preserved, and visit buildings that have had many changes in use throughout their existence. When you enter a space to work with your clairsalience, just relax, get into that daydreamy theta state, and inhale with your nose.

KEEP IN MIND: As with any of these abilities, if you smell the same mysterious smell constantly, you would be wise to get checked out by a doctor. What you're looking for with clairsalience is trends—for example, if every time a passed loved one pops into your mind you suddenly start smelling their cologne, that's clairsalience. However, if you're *constantly* smelling cologne, that may not be psychic.

Clairgustance: "I Taste . . ."

WHAT IT IS: Clairgustance is psychic taste. This is the most uncommon psychic skill; however, it is common with those who have a passion for cooking and baking. People who have natural clairsalience may also have clairgustance and not be aware of it. After all, our noses are directly connected to our tongues. If you're already thinking, *What's the use of that?*, I'll give you a few examples.

HOW TO USE IT: If you've ever tried to recall what something tasted like after many years of not having it, or if you're trying to recreate an old family recipe that you've never had, you can use clairgustance. If you're connecting with your own memory of a food you enjoyed or maybe even a food you hated, trust your tongue to be able to recall the memory to communicate it to you. I've used the skill of clairgustance with a ghost. I asked him what his favorite kind of alcohol was. I got a light, tart taste on the back of my tongue, as if I were tasting the seltzer version of the real thing. After some research, I found out that what I was chasing was a kind of gooseberry liquor. I had never had gooseberry before, but I was able to find out about what it would've tasted like through other people's experiences.

Examples:

- Being able to taste something in detail without having had it before.
- Going into the kitchen or dining room of a historic site and being able to taste what used to be made or served there.

ACTIVITY: You can build this skill in the physical world by tasting complex foods and trying to identify the ingredients, then checking your senses. Take this as your excuse to enjoy some great food! Something I do on a regular basis is ask my passed grandmother to come in and help me cook. As she's been passed on for almost a decade now and my memory of her food is more about emotion than about flavors, I ask her to give me her opinion on what I cook from the other side. Throughout the process of cooking, I sample the food and then send the taste to her, just as if I were sharing a spiritual spoon with her. She then sends me a taste back based on what I need to add to the dish to make it more like hers. This can be a great way to connect with your ancestors as well!

KEEP IN MIND: As with clairsalience, if you're tasting something all the time, or if everything tastes bitter, or if you don't taste anything at all, you may have a medical issue that you should consider going to see a doctor about.

GHOST STORY

THE BLOODY ROAD

This story will show you how I used several of my psychic senses on what I thought was just an unassuming cobblestone street in historic Charleston, South Carolina. Tharyn had recently been to Charleston and had learned of its highly haunted history on one of the many ghost tours available. In comparison, I knew next to nothing of the city's specific ghosts—only that it was reputed to be haunted.

An intuitive activity I like to do when traveling with my partner is to find areas where I feel something may have happened. I asked Tharyn to walk with me around the oldest parts of the city, and to take me to places they had visited on their ghost tour but not to give me any information about what had happened there. At each spot they led me to, I took some time to tune into what I was picking up on and then presented my perceptions to Tharyn. Tharyn would then tell me what history they knew of the spot, and I would compare those stories to my reads.

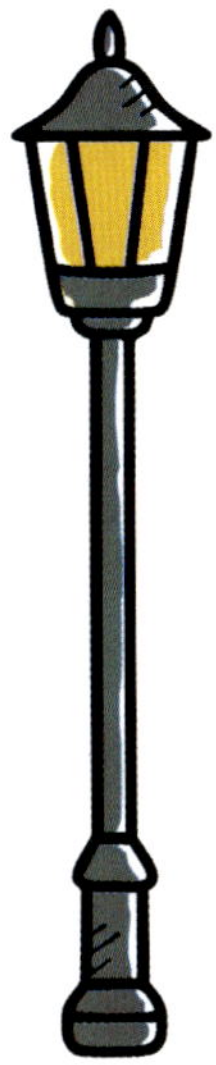

One street in particular radiated energy that I could feel even before we got there. All the other streets we walked on seemed well lit and easy to navigate. As we turned left, I felt the energy get thick. It seemed to get colder the farther we went. I stopped. Tharyn smiled knowingly. They told me to tell them what I was feeling. Immediately I knew that people had been shot and murdered here—and it wasn't a one-time occurrence.

The sounds came next. At first the pressure on my ears made me feel like I was under water. I readjusted my energetic balance and dove in, this time doing what I could to move through and past what I was hearing. Hooves of horses. Carriages moving behind some of them. A woman screaming. A guttural "Ugh!" as if someone had been hit in the stomach. For a moment I felt the idea of an impact on my own stomach. I readjusted and released it. Whatever that was, whoever that was, I was not interested in taking on the energy of their ultimate end.

The unmistakable smell of blood hit the back of my nose. I could almost taste it on my tongue, it was so strong. I adjusted and released. All the while, I slowly nudged my way back toward the street we had just come from. Even though the cobblestone street had lights on it, I couldn't get past the feeling that it was darker. It just felt darker.

The hairs on the back of my neck were standing up. A feeling of needing to watch my back grew. The nervousness followed. Moving in the darkness, was I seeing shadows that slipped just behind corners whenever I focused on them? Even as I knew no one living was behind me, I wanted to keep turning around. My senses were navigating an overload of information all coming in at once and all adding up to one overwhelming feeling.

Once I'd taken in all of these sensations, I quelled the feelings around me and got back to my balance. I took a breath and told Tharyn I was ready to learn the history of the place. They told me that we were standing on what had been nicknamed The Bloody Road. It was the only road in town where, for a time, all crime had been legal. Duels took place. Pickpockets roamed. People were stabbed. No one ever wanted to be caught on The Bloody Road. Even after the laws extended to that street, the feelings of all that had once transpired there continued.

IN SUMMARY

People who are receiving psychic information often do not understand that that's happening, because they do not know how to break down how they perceive spiritual interactions. In understanding the seven psychic senses and how all of them can be grown, you clear the way for trusting your natural intuition. Get playful in your psychic exploration by using the activities in this chapter and making some up for yourself!

HERE ARE SOME KEY POINTS TO REMEMBER:

- When you feel that a ghost may be around, notice what each psychic sense is feeling.
    - **Claircognizance:** I know information I didn't know before.
    - **Clairvoyance:** I see images that are beyond the physical plane.
    - **Clairaudience:** I hear spiritual information and energy.
    - **Clairtangency/Psychometry:** I physically feel spiritual interactions.
    - **Clairemotion/Clairsentience:** I emotionally feel shifts in people and entities around me.
    - **Clairsalience:** I smell spiritual energy.
    - **Clairgustance:** I taste psychic information.

CHAPTER 6

HOW TO START A CONVERSATION WITH A GHOST

Up until this point in the book, you have been preparing for your spiritual experiences. Now it's time to put all that information into practice. In this chapter, you will learn how to start a grounded conversation with a spirit. You'll go over how to treat a ghost with respect, with the intention that they may want to communicate with you for more than just a few words. You'll also learn how to communicate with spirits in a confident way while maintaining groundedness and integrity.

PREPARING FOR GHOSTLY CONVERSATIONS

In the moment you meet a spirit, it can be surprisingly easy to forget basic human interaction skills. I highly recommend having some questions laid out beforehand that you can ask the spirits you interact with. Make the questions fun and engaging, because the better the question, the more likely the spirits will want to talk.

You may also want to bring along items that you think the ghosts would enjoy. For example, if you're going to a place where there may be ghosts of children, you may like to bring some old-fashioned toys for them to play with. If you're going to an old jail or house from the turn of the century, you may want to bring cigarettes and booze to share with anybody who would like to talk. Sharing food and other offerings without expectation of anyone having to talk to you may be just the ticket to getting spirits to open up. To share items with spirits, simply lay the items out on an easily accessible table or clean middle-ground space and invite the spirits to partake in consuming them as they would have in life. Occasionally the items may move. Sometimes they'll even disappear. At minimum, their color, smell, and taste are likely to lose their luster once the items' essence has been consumed.

It's also a good idea to be ready to write down the psychic senses you find yourself using as you visit with spirits. Throughout your interactions, ask yourself *how* you're perceiving information. Sometimes you may forget how you are perceiving things until you intentionally remind yourself to notice it—and you may forget to attend to other psychic senses. For example, you may pick up on a clairsalient scent.

Unless you're intentionally noticing which senses you're using, you may forget to tap into the emotion: How did that scent make the spirit feel? Did the smell of horses excite the ghost nearby? Or was it a sign of another day of work, which made them tired?

GHOSTLY GO-TO

The word *ghost* is related to the Old English word *gast*, which can mean "spirit" or "soul." The first record we have of the word *ghost* being used as we do today—meaning "a soul of someone who has passed, in visible form"—is from the fourteenth century.

With everything prepared, it's time to get to chatting! Remember: Time with spirits can be limited, so utilize what sources of information you need to, but otherwise just start. Ideally, you'll have a place where you won't be rushed for time and it will be quiet enough for you to not only hear your thoughts but also be able to make out someone else's on the other side. However, when life happens to put you in a space with a spirit, you can't always control the environment. Remind yourself that you can always control *you* and your needs. Everything else is a lesson to learn.

KEYS TO CONVERSATION

The following are some step-by-step tips on how to start your spirit communication. After a few experiences connecting with ghosts, you will find what works best for you and in what order. For now, here are the steps I recommend for your ghostly conversations:

Step One: Mindfulness and Cleansing

A spiritual connection outside of you must first start *with* you. That doesn't mean you have to have a flawless day. It doesn't mean that you need to be perfectly hydrated. However, in order to best understand the spiritual information that you will be receiving psychically, you must first connect with yourself. This may mean taking a moment for mindfulness and to cleanse your energy of anything that's not yours before you go to a haunted location. It may also mean, once you get to the haunted location (whether or not you knew you'd be going to said haunted location), to take a quiet private moment to check in with yourself. Remember: Checking in with where you're at allows you to give the best unbiased read possible. You don't want your own feelings and experiences to muddy up the connection you may have with someone new. (Refer to Chapters 3 and 4 to practice your mindfulness and cleansing techniques.)

Step Two: Grounding and Shielding

Whenever possible, you should ground your energy and shield yourself before going to any haunted location.

Granted, sometimes you don't always have the chance to do that *before* you get to a location, but once you're there, if you haven't already, you should take a quiet moment to yourself to protect your personal energetic space. It doesn't matter how excited everyone else may be around you—your first responsibility is to yourself. Never let anyone else keep you from protecting yourself or your energy. (Refer to Chapter 4 for information on shielding.)

Step Three: Prepare for the Physical

Remember that if your physical body is unhappy, your spiritual perception will likely be just as unhappy, if not more so. If you're going to be outside, be sure to check the weather before you go. Nothing dampens the mood more than being physically cold or wet or in poor footwear. Also, be sure that the place you're going to allows you to be there legally. Constantly having concerns about the police or untrustworthy people showing up will cause your intuition to focus more on physical safety than on spiritual connection. If it's going to be dark, pack a flashlight, and be sure to pack extra batteries, as sometimes they can lose power quickly around spirits.

Step Four: Questions Upon Arrival

The caretakers of some historic locations are leery about people connecting with their ghosts. If you are concerned the site you are going to will not welcome you, you can either check for information online or ask someone who works there if it would be okay to connect with spirits in that place. Often, if you kindly explain that you're looking to further understand history and intend to treat the spirits with the utmost respect, most staff will not mind you quietly doing your thing. And this bears repeating: Upon arriving, do a quick check-in with your energy before expanding your awareness to the energy around you. You'll want to be able to ask yourself, *What changed as I walked in here?* If you don't start at your base level, you won't know where you're at or where you're going!

GHOSTLY GO-TO

Some shows and movies that portray casual ghostly conversations include but are not limited to BBC's *Ghosts*, CBS's *Ghosts*, the movies *Casper* and *The Ghost and Mrs. Muir*, and Disney's cartoon series *The Ghost and Molly McGee.*

Step Five: Get Daydreamy

Once you're in the location and ready to start, take a nice deep breath and do whatever you need to do to relax. Relax your vision, loosen your shoulders, and take another good breath. Let your mind drift. Remind yourself that you're safe. Seep into that supposedly imaginative world. If you get a little tired, that's okay—it's a good sign that you're relaxing into the theta state. This is where you're going to want to be to make your readings. If your feelings ever get intense or overwhelming and the intensity begins to clog your ability to perceive, remember that you can always go back to your balanced base point, just as you can always go back to any of the previous steps as needed.

Step Six: Write Down Everything

Take five to ten minutes to write down or take note of every sensation you're having. This is when you ask yourself what has changed around you since you arrived at the haunted location. Utilize your seven psychic senses. Ask yourself, *What am I sensing?* Allow your perception to drift and find natural interest in different areas. A natural disinterest in a particular area could also be a psychic perception. You can always make note of it without having to read into it, especially if it makes you uncomfortable. Not wanting to explore a particular area can be validated by information you look up later, just as choosing to explore an area can be.

Even when your mind doesn't seem to come up with anything new, keep asking, *Is there anything else?* Write down even the small things. It's always better to have more written down than not have enough—or, worse, to have thought or felt something and to have ignored it rather than writing it down. In order to build up confidence in your metaphysical perceptions, you need to have proof of your ability, in the form of a record in the physical world. That's why notetaking is so important, especially over time.

Step Seven: Follow Your Intuition

Now you get to decide where it is you want to go. Perhaps you feel drawn to a particular room. As long as you have permission to go there, you should go. Perhaps there's a presence you want to explore. See if the presence wants to connect with you. If you're only perceiving in one way, you can always ask yourself, *What else am I sensing with my other psychic senses?* For example, even if you're not emotionally feeling anything, you can always ask yourself, *If there were an emotion to feel, what would it be?* Remember that people and ghosts speak in many ways, not just audibly. Sometimes it's with a nod or a shake of the head. Sometimes it's with a step backward. Sometimes it's with a handshake. Think of the everyday interactions that you would have with other living people; ghosts may be using those same methods.

GHOSTLY GO-TO

The studies of psychology, anthropology, and historical linguistics can be very beneficial in helping you understand your spiritual connections. Acting and improv classes can help you better read and observe mannerisms and body language as well.

Step Eight: Cleanse and Close Out

Whether you need to take a break or you need to leave for the day, cleansing and closing out are important. This step can be as simple as letting everything and everyone around you know that you're leaving and that no one is allowed to follow you. You may want to use a tool such as a smoke cleanse or a water cleanse, as long as those things are allowed in your location. You can also do a quick cleanse before getting in your car and leaving. Whatever you do, be sure that your intention is clear. Just as you wouldn't let a stranger in the physical world follow you home, so you shouldn't let a stranger in the spirit realm follow you home either. It's important to stay safe. You can always have further spiritual experiences later and in locations where your personal space is not compromised.

GHOST STORY

THE REMOVED ENTITY

It is only through my years of experience that I've become able to provide spirits with the amount of patience and calm understanding that I now can. Sometimes, it takes a lot of effort to put the feeling of fear aside for the pursuit of sympathetic understanding. Just as I try to treat each client with patience (they're trying to understand what their brain tells them is physically impossible!), I try to be sympathetic to spirits who need help. However, that's not to say that every ghost ought to go entirely unchecked. Compromise can and ought to be part of any situation, such as in this story, where I helped a client identify and sympathize with a lost spirit.

I once met with a client who had a lot of concerns regarding the spirit she had interacted with in her basement. She told me that her house was in a new development and before the neighborhood was there it had been wooded land. I could tell that whatever was going on had really shaken her. When she mentioned the way her two younger kids had reacted, I began to grow concerned. Before she could finish telling me about all of what she had been experiencing, I kindly asked her to pause so that I could look into the situation myself.

Since the consultation was virtual, I asked for her consent to look into the situation using astral projection and claircognizance. She agreed, and I was off. In the basement, I picked up on some worn-in, mismatched sofas that were in an *L* shape facing a large television. Beside the TV was a corner that looked darker to me than it ought to have been. There was nothing wrong or odd about the corner itself; it had inset shelves holding some DVDs and a few odds and ends. Then I saw him.

The ghost couldn't have been more than eighteen. He wore a loose-fitting, white tracksuit jacket with a red stripe going down the sleeve, with a simple white T-shirt underneath. For pants, he had light jeans, and he wore sneakers. He had bags under his eyes as if he were constantly tired. When I revealed myself, he stepped back into the shelves. I called to him before he left.

Through a bit of conversation, I explained why I was there and who had called me in. I asked if he knew where he was. He shrugged. I asked if he knew who the family was. He said, "Not really." I asked if he had lived in the house before. He shook his head. I asked what he thought about the family. He said he liked them and he liked when they would watch movies and play video games together. I then asked the uncomfortable question: *Did he know what happened to him?*

I got the indication he knew he was a spirit. I saw mental imagery of him standing over his body right after he passed. There was a car wreck. He had been with friends. I then saw him going back to his family. I saw pictures of him being taken off of their walls. The house looked nothing like the one the woman lived in, but I got the indication it wasn't too far away. Through the boy's eyes, I saw him trying to connect with his mother through her grief, but whenever he did, she would get scared. The next image I got was of a priest going through the home. The priest had his parents rebuke his spirit and call him a demon preying on their sadness. The boy left, and I saw random images of his journey. Next was a memory of the present family eating snacks and watching a show. I felt him smile and move toward them. One of the kids looked at him and nearly started crying. He didn't know what the child saw—only that seeing him made the child very upset.

"I didn't mean to scare him," he told me. "For a second I thought he was my younger brother . . . then I remembered everything."

His story made me want to cry. I relayed this to the client. I told her that the ghost's energy likely felt scary because he was confused. The client then confirmed that there were a few older houses at the other end of their street that the boy may have lived at. She said she didn't know anyone who lived there. From the looks of things, by the time of our conversation, the ghost's parents would have been elderly.

I asked the ghost if he wanted to move on or go somewhere else. I could see tears in his eyes as he asked if he could stay. He said he really liked the family and he never meant to scare them. He'd picked a corner where he thought he would be out of the way. The client, the ghost, and I devised a compromise. When the kids were downstairs, he had to tuck himself farther away so they

wouldn't be scared. The client, in her compassion, offered to try and talk with him when she could. That seemed to make him very hopeful.

By the time of the follow-up consultation, I could tell the energy was already a lot better. I had given the client some personalized tips on communicating with the ghost based on the natural intuitive inclinations she already had. The kids had not gotten scared since our last conversation. The ghost seemed very content, and the bags under his eyes were nearly gone. I hope they're still doing just as well.

TREATING GHOSTS WITH RESPECT

What does it really mean to treat ghosts with respect? Does it mean leaving them alone and disengaging entirely? Does it mean allowing them to do whatever they please, even if it disrupts your peace? Or does it mean thinking you can move them on to a better place based on your perception that they don't belong with us at all? Many people will take the approach that ghosts only deserve respect when the ghosts are performing for them—as if the ghosts owe something to the living just for existing. That always seemed strange to me. If we assume that ghosts were once human, why are they suddenly treated inhumanly once they're out of their bodies?

As for me and the approach that I take with spirits, it's as relaxed as possible. I ground my connections in the same ethics and morals that I do with the living. The same boundaries I have with living people, I have with anything else that comes my way. Ghosts are not there for my entertainment, just as I am not there for their annoyance. Here are some elements that I recommend keeping in mind as you decide how to treat any spirits you encounter.

Permission

Once you pick up on the fact that you're in a haunted place, or upon entering a haunted place, state out loud (or as an unsaid, projected thought that goes out and around you like its own sound wave) that you have permission to be where you are. Tell whoever may be listening who gave you the permission, and that you're there to acknowledge and better understand anyone else who may be sharing the location or building with you. If you're merely a visitor or patron of an establishment, say as much. If you're about to move in or are already living there, say that.

Intentions

Let any nearby spirits know what you're there to do, even if it's just to eat with friends. Offering basic information like this can put them at ease. Think about it: If someone you didn't know walked into your private office at work, wouldn't you be a little on edge until they told you what they were doing there? Introduce yourself. If you're looking for something or someone in particular, let them know. A little communication and consideration can go a long way. It allows the spirit to feel like they are in control of whether or not they want to be involved with your time there. This simple sharing of information can create great ease for everyone involved.

Conversation

Would you walk into a place you've never been and ask a person you'd never met before to tell you about the most traumatic time in their life? Would you demand they tell you their name and their innermost secrets? I would hope not! Don't do this with ghosts either! There are other clarifying questions you can ask of a spirit to get the answers you're looking for. Let's say a ghost was a baker. Ask them what kind of pastry felt like a chore and what sort of cake they most enjoyed baking. If you think you've seen a ghost, either clairvoyantly or through a photo, ask them to confirm or deny their various physical attributes.

If a ghost wants attention, they'll tell you whatever they think you want to hear. For example, if you ask, "Were you behind the murder?" and they respond with a resounding "Yes!" they may be doing that to get personal entertainment from your reaction. If you want to know who you're talking to, ask them everyday questions about things that the person who you're actually looking for would have known. While spirits may not always remember all the details about their lives, looks, and interests, if you really want quantifiable connections with spirits, ask them the questions they may not be expecting.

The key to ongoing conversation is to know when to pivot. If you aren't getting any answers on a specific topic, change topics. Sometimes it helps to get silly and ask questions that are funny and pointless. Remember: You're meeting someone new. Don't you want them to feel like they can be their authentic self in order to create and share a real connection? People skills and a little bit of psychology knowledge can go a long way here.

Boundaries and Action

In the event you get attention you were not looking for or don't want, remember that boundaries stated must be backed up with action. Even if the ghost isn't trying to hurt you, if they do by accident, you don't have to stick around for it. For example, let's say a spirit is getting really confused and that feeling begins to give you a splitting headache every time you're near them. While their confusion may be something the ghost needs to sort through on their own, you don't have to stick around for it. You can always kindly communicate that their energy is making you feel dizzy and you would like to get back to your personal balance before continuing conversation.

GHOSTLY GO-TO

Cultures have a variety of beliefs in regard to whether ghosts are good, evil, or neither. Mexico's Day of the Dead is one of various holidays around the world that celebrate and revere the spirits of ancestors.

On the other hand, if a spirit is specifically trying to target you to make you feel uncomfortable—whether that be through mental imagery, whispered cruelties, or attempts to physically harm you—leave! If your friend were in an abusive situation, would you tell them to stick with it and try to prove something about themselves? Be your own friend here. You have nothing to prove by putting up with abuse. Leave. You can always return once you've grown more comfortable with your shielding. Until then, take care of yourself.

GHOST STORY

THE LESS INTERESTED GHOSTS

It's important to treat ghosts with respect. Not all ghosts want to talk to the people who are looking to talk to them. Some ghosts, especially those in famously haunted locations, just want to be left alone. A psychic medium coming into their sphere is not always exciting for them. I was reminded of this fact when I visited the infamous Jennie Wade House in Gettysburg, Pennsylvania.

It was my first official paranormal investigation as a psychic medium. Despite having quantifiable experiences from the past, I was concerned that what I could offer to the team for the night might not be verifiable enough for their standards. On top of that, I had no one to remind me to check my energy or even to pack a heavier coat. It was after midnight (which is well past my bedtime), and I was cold and nervous, but I still showed up.

As the house is a top tourist destination for paranormal investigators of all levels of experience, a group had already entered the house before mine. As the group before ours left, I saw that its members were clearly looking to be scared. Their energy was all over the place. They were loud. They were playing jokes on each other. They didn't come off as being particularly interested in the history or the individual spirits themselves. I wanted to make as much distance as possible between our group and the previous one. Once inside, the investigators in my group proposed that I go from room to room and make psychic reads that I could present to them later. I was unfamiliar with the history of the house, and I was looking forward to the challenge.

As I stepped into the parlor, I got the immediate feeling that someone was angry. I tuned in to discover an elderly man sitting in an armchair. He was grumbling about his displeasure about the furniture in the room. He wanted things to be relocated to suit his personal interests. He did not seem the least bit interested in me. Wanting to learn more about him, in addition to wanting to know if his presence there was a common occurrence for other tourists, I reached out and asked him if he would talk to me.

The old man was quick to tell me he did not want to talk. I pressed a little bit more. He grumbled again. I asked if there was something I could do to help his situation. He asked if I could rearrange the furniture and replace his chair with a nicer chair. I told him I was unable to do that. He then told me—in not so many words—that he was not interested in talking to me and I would help him the most by leaving.

I got this same feeling from many other spirits at the Jennie Wade House. While I am certain there are individuals the spirits enjoy interacting with, most of the spirits I ran into that night were uninterested in connecting. It may have had to do with the boisterous group that toured the house before mine. Or it may have had to do with the reality that this small house never gets any time of rest or peace. (It's not only open for investigations on a nightly basis; it's also open throughout the day as a gift shop.)

While I was looking forward to speaking with spirits there, I had to put my wants aside. Spirits deserve respect. I could still make my psychic reads without necessarily needing to use my mediumship and mediator skills. I think it's unfair to force ghosts to talk for our enjoyment and entertainment. The older man only came forward due to his displeasure with the furniture. What would be the good of bothering him—or any of the other spirits—further? They already had enough going on as it was.

COMMUNICATING WITH CONFIDENCE

To be clear: Communicating with confidence does not mean being rude or pushy. Think of what confidence looks like in other people. How does it make you feel? What actions do you take to feel more confident? How do you think you make others feel when you act this way? What is it about your words and actions that keep people coming back to want to connect with you again?

What works with people works the same way for ghosts. No two ghosts are exactly alike. Some may take a liking to you, whereas others may want nothing to do with you. How you carry yourself will make a statement not only about what kind of treatment you're looking to give but also about what you're willing to receive.

GHOST STORY

"WHY DIDN'T THEY RUN?"

I still find myself in a world surrounded by people who say that I should be afraid of ghosts. While I can't speak for everyone, I find that when people say this to me they're often speaking of their own fears. I used to let their fears directly paint my own, because I felt that I didn't know any better. Now, having met hundreds of spirits, I find myself drawn to revisiting the very experiences that led to the level of confidence I have today.

A few years ago I hosted an in-person event for my exclusive online community. We met in the oldest colonial town in the United States, St. Augustine, Florida. Due to high interest from the group, the trip organizer booked us an investigation at St. Augustine's old jail, which is one of the most famously haunted places in this famously haunted city. Personally, I was less than enthused.

Something to understand about me is that I'm used to being surrounded by ghosts. I gravitate to living in cities where ghosts are never hard to find. Going to a famously haunted hotspot doesn't have the same excitement and appeal for me as it might for most people who don't live in such supernatural places. In addition to this, I'm very picky about which old jails, hospitals, and asylums I visit. Many of these places have seen enough hardship. The people who linger there have enough to deal with. I don't want my presence and the poking-and-prodding nature of a paranormal investigation to make their situation any worse than it already is.

For the old jail, I made an exception and went along with the group. I didn't know why at the time, but I felt like the energy I would run into wouldn't be entirely gloomy and overly visited like some of the other high-tourist areas. I trusted my intuition and was pleasantly surprised by most of the encounters I had.

Since I was leading the group to better connect with their intuitive abilities, I led everyone through an exercise similar to one that I've previously laid out in this book. I had everyone match with a balance and cross-validation buddy for safety (meaning that the small groups would work together to remind each other to check in to balance their energy, as well as making reads for themselves to check in with each other's reads). I reminded everyone that we were not there to feed into the fear. We were there to make genuine connections and to learn about the real stories of the ghosts that were there.

At the beginning we all split up and agreed to meet back up later to compare reads and notes. During this time I did a bit of energetic cleansing so that energy could move around a bit more. I did my own reads into the rooms where we were told "demons" existed. I felt eyes watching, and there were some pretty intimidating spirits to talk to, but I didn't let them get to me. I stood my ground and treated them as I would treat anyone, alive or dead. The spirits were confused at my approach, but otherwise they didn't try to push my boundaries.

When we joined up again, many in the group had experiences that were both psychic and investigative to share. We all gathered around a Phasmabox (described in Chapter 7) and asked the nearby ghosts to talk to us. Everything was casual, despite some of the spirits trying to scare us. Feeling like we were in on a joke that worked on most tourists coming in, we asked them to give us all they'd got.

A loud roar came through the speakers.

We all looked at each other, then excitedly started to applaud and compliment the ghosts on their effort.

A quieter voice came through: "Why didn't they run?"

It was then that I realized why I'd felt it was okay to visit. The ghosts seemed to *like* what they did to scare guests. They enjoyed being a part of the theatrics; they felt important. For the first time maybe ever—in life or death—the general public was excited to see them just for them. They were no longer outcasts of society. They were celebrities. All they had to do to maintain their status was play the haunting game.

Once we all shared the same understanding, we were able to have some more casual conversation. We asked the ghosts about their interests, what they liked to do for fun, and if they were happy enough where they were. It was a very enlightening time for everyone.

CLOSING OUT AND CLEANSING

You wouldn't leave a place without closing the door. Of course not! So why would you exit from a highly energetic space without doing the same? The good news is closing out and cleansing your energy does not have to be a long, drawn-out affair as long as you are thorough with your intentions.

At a minimum level, you need to state clearly, "No one is allowed to follow me." At a maximum level, you're welcome to create a song-and-dance number with lit incense sticks in your hands. And yes, I've seen both versions. Sometimes the latter will ensure the ghosts do not want to follow you home, because you'll probably look pretty crazy to them. But, a cleanse is a cleanse, right?

Whatever you do, I recommend using elements that have already been working for you when cleansing. For example, as I tend to couple a smoke cleanse with my energy work, I usually have a few incense sticks waiting in the car after visiting a highly haunted spot. As I move the incense around my body, I imagine any potential lines of paranormal energy that may have latched onto me either with or without my awareness are singed by the incense and returned to wherever they belong.

GHOSTLY GO-TO

Music can be a natural way to cleanse. You can make a cleanse-and-recharge playlist that gives you a freeing feeling whenever you listen to it. You may want to include songs with themes of breaking chains, resetting or redemption, and moving forward. Singing and dancing can be a great cleanse, especially when there's intention behind it. Get creative!

If you find yourself particularly drained after your connections, you may need to reclaim your energy. I recommend standing with feet flat, taking a slow deep breath, and speaking to the energy around you. You can say whatever resonates with you. I will sometimes say, "I reclaim all energy that leaked from me either consciously or unconsciously. As I breathe in, it returns now and with nothing besides my energy attached to it." Take a breath, give your energy a color, and see that color flowing back into you with your mind's eye.

Dealing with the Fatigue

Sometimes tapping into your psychic skills can get tiresome; after all, you really are activating a muscle. If you find you have a headache around your third eye or forehead, be sure you're hydrated and take any needed medications. You don't have to sit in discomfort! There are no medals for being in pain when you don't have to be.

Sometimes psychics and investigators alike experience "investigation hangovers," feeling very tired the day after a spiritual interaction. A few different factors may lead to this drowsiness:

- The obvious one is that you have probably been up all night with hardly any sleep.
- It could be that some ghosts have taken a portion of your energy.
- And finally, you may feel exhausted from tapping into your intuition and psychic abilities when you typically don't do this on a day-to-day basis.

There doesn't *need* to be a hangover or a drained feeling after connecting with spirits. To get ahead of the exhaustion, listen to your body and its needs in real time. Sometimes, despite your best efforts, you'll still get tired—you're human. Do what you can to take care of yourself. Sometimes that just means taking an easy day to stay in bed and sleep the day after a spiritual interaction. All things considered, I hope you take whatever excuse you need to grant yourself some well-deserved rest!

GHOST STORY

THE TETHERED GHOSTS

While anyone can jump into the pursuit of paranormal communication, if you don't take a moment to check in with your own energy, it becomes very easy for spirits to follow you. People are naturally good at adapting to carrying extra physical weight, and carrying ghosts can sometimes work in the same way. However, just because you *can* carry the energy, it doesn't mean you should have to, especially when you may have no idea who's trailing behind. This is a story of how one of my clients discovered he was carrying some unknown weight.

Every so often, a highly experienced paranormal investigator will book a consultation with me. It's always fun to swap stories about different places we've been. They often want to learn what psychic abilities they may be able to utilize to have the best investigations possible. I always love having conversations like this—especially as many paranormal investigators have never before been taught that it's possible to be both an investigator and a medium. I get to share with them that the two roles don't have to counteract each other. However, because many investigators have been taught few or no spiritual hygienic practices, I sometimes find stowaways on their energy from the sites they've visited.

One client I met with had—I kid you not—*eighteen ghosts* trailing his energy. He had been ghost hunting for years and was very passionate about what he did. Over the years, he began to notice that more of his technology spiked in readings wherever he went. It didn't matter if he was at a haunted site or at home, whenever he had his gadgets on they always signaled *ghost* around him. At first, this was really exciting evidence for him . . . until he realized that it wasn't just the places he was visiting that were haunted. *He* was haunted, and it was beginning to have a negative effect on his everyday life.

The stories accumulated over time. At first it was a heavy feeling in his house. Then it was dreams where he saw various deaths that weren't his own. Cold spots began to collect around him, and other people sometimes picked up on them. His relationship with his girlfriend was suffering because, after waking up to a ghost staring at her, she no longer wanted to stay the night with him. He found himself exhausted most of the time. He was losing control.

On top of all of this, many of the ghosts hadn't meant to latch onto his energy the way they had. Some were angry and were very expressive about wanting to leave. I had to talk to each one, one at a time, as many began to talk over one another. In speaking with the different spirits, I checked information with the client. He confirmed that the places I was seeing from the ghosts' perspective were places he had visited in the past.

Eight ghosts were sent back to where they came from. Three ghosts decided they didn't want to stay on this plane anymore, so I assisted them with that transition. Two ghosts wanted my client to return to where he'd picked them up so that they could show him something near their gravesite. The remaining five ghosts enjoyed traveling with him and asked to stay. Some of them even felt protective of him. However, as two of those ghosts were taking too much energy from him, I ultimately made the decision to return them to where they came from. That left three ghosts.

I taught the ghosts how to harness their own energy rather than taking it from the client. I also checked with the client that it would be okay with him if they stayed. We had a long talk on consent and boundaries, especially related to the ghosts' behavior around guests in his house. I also had an even longer talk with the client about being more responsible with where his energy was going during investigations. Ghosts don't always know that they're taking energy from us; it's our own responsibility to keep our energy balanced and safe.

Sadly, this client did not take my advice to heart. When I met with him for his follow-up, he had three new ghosts in tow. I asked if he had been cleansing his energy like we talked about. He told me he hadn't been because he kept forgetting. He then

said that he thought it was cool that the ghosts wanted to follow him, even when it was having a negative effect on his everyday life and health. I repeated my warnings to him and he said he understood. I never saw or heard from him again.

IN SUMMARY

To communicate with ghosts, you draw on the same kinds of techniques you use when communicating with the living. However, as you do not perceive spirits the same way, it's necessary to take extra precautions in how you handle yourself when you're looking to meet them. Following these protocols is the way to have safe, authentic, and memorable experiences that don't feel out of your control.

HERE ARE SOME KEY POINTS TO REMEMBER:

- Prepare for your conversation by staying mindful, cleansing beforehand, grounding your energy, and shielding.
- Be sure that you're physically safe whenever you connect with spirits, and ask any necessary questions before you begin your psychic work.
- Once in theta state, write down everything you experience.
- Follow your intuition.
- Don't forget to cleanse and close out before leaving.
- Treat ghosts with respect by letting them know you have permission to be there, stating your intentions, having considerate conversations, and keeping your boundaries in place.

CHAPTER 7

CROSS-VALIDATING WITH TOOLS

People have long been trying to get "proof" to help justify and validate their spiritual experiences. Fortunately, today we live in a time of great technological advancement, which has not only helped people debunk their fears—it's also helped them quantify their psychic experiences. In this chapter you'll learn about the technological tools for connecting with ghosts and how easy it can be to use them. You'll also explore some older tools for psychic validation that have been used for thousands of years—and discover how to connect with them safely.

TECHNOLOGY TOOLS

The following are tried-and-true paranormal investigation tools that:

- Won't break your bank.
- Are relatively easy to find and buy.
- Will couple well with your growing ability to trust your psychic skill sets.

Reach for these tools *after* you've made your psychic reads. If you use them from the beginning, you may end up trusting the tool more than your own natural abilities. Also, remember that you won't always have these items with you, but you'll always have your psychic skills. Don't let overreliance on tools take away your natural ability to connect with spiritual activity around you. However, if you are in a situation where you have access to these tools, they can support your psychic reads.

Flashlight

WHAT IT IS: Any kind of flashlight with a button or switch.

HOW TO USE IT: Either turn the beam on and ask the ghost to turn it off or turn it off and ask the ghost to turn it on.

Example: *"Spirit, if you love dancing, can you turn the light on?"*

KEEP IN MIND: Be sure to have spare batteries with you. Too much on and off can kill batteries. Ghosts can also drain batteries—they may be a useful energy source for them.

TROUBLESHOOTING: Not all ghosts automatically know how to work a flashlight, especially if they're not in touch with modern technology. If you feel confusion (which, remember, might be the spirit's emotion, picked up on through clairemotion), explain how it works: If the spirit takes up space on the flashlight by standing or sitting on it or by gripping the flashlight really tightly, the light may turn on with surges of emotion. This activity may be tiring for spirits trying it for the first time. If the beam is not going on and off, it may be because the spirit is having difficulty gathering enough energy to affect the flashlight.

Camera and Recorder

WHAT IT IS: A cell phone that has both video and audio recording capability will do just fine here, although you can get as high-tech as you like. I recommend recording both audio and video so that you can see and hear what happened when you're reviewing your evidence.

HOW TO USE IT: Having a tripod or monopod for ease is ideal, but as long as you set your phone or other recorder up in a space where there's a clear line of sight and the microphone isn't muffled, you're good. I recommend using horizontal recording for a better view around you.

KEEP IN MIND: Have a charger on hand! Ghosts will drain phone, camera, and recorder batteries. If you're going to livestream, remember that high-energy spirits can also affect cell signals. It may help to ask the ghosts to stay away from your recording equipment.

TROUBLESHOOTING: If you're going to be in the dark, bring a light. If you want to use night-vision applications, understand their quality may be poor. I don't recommend using phone apps that supposedly create imagery of spirits behind and around you. They often add to apprehension and take away from legitimate psychic connection and investigation.

GHOSTLY GO-TO

The age of the original instant-photo Polaroid cameras was said to be a golden age for spotting ghosts through technology. People reported seeing unexplained streaks of light, orbs or light balls, and full apparitions. However, the validity of such photos is still debated.

Touch Lights (Light-Up Cat Toys)

WHAT THEY ARE: Typically, a touch light is a little plastic ball with a red button. When the button is pushed, red and blue lights come on inside the clear plastic ball. Set it down and leave it alone, and the lights turn off. When contact is made with the ball, the lights go on again.

HOW TO USE THEM: Similarly to when using flashlights, you may need to explain to the spirits how these balls work and that they won't hurt them. I've met spirits who are very uncertain about these balls because the lights are too flashy for them. I like to place a bunch of balls all around me or in places where there may be a lot of ghosts walking. I've seen balls go off one after the other as if someone walked through them.

KEEP IN MIND: Some spirits find this form of communication demeaning. Just as you may want to have a straightforward conversation, they may want to do the same. Remind them that you're working on your communication and that tools such as these help you.

TROUBLESHOOTING: If you feel a ghost is really trying but having trouble operating the lights, tell them to stomp on them or run through them. Consider playing some music that may excite the ghost. The energy of the excitement can help them affect the lights.

Electromagnetic Field (EMF) Meter

WHAT IT IS: EMF meters are used to check for safe levels of electromagnetic waves in buildings. To be sure yours is working, turn it on and go to an electrical outlet or lamp. You'll see the lights on the top of the wand move up and down depending on how close you are to the electrical current.

HOW TO USE IT: These work similarly to touch lights and flashlights; however, I've found them to be even more effective. EMF readers are not as exhausting for ghosts to use, because ghosts don't have to do much besides stand or sit on or near the meter. Often, the more excited a ghost is regarding a subject, the higher the lights will flash. This can be great for asking yes and no questions. Yes answers will likely get higher readings on the meter.

KEEP IN MIND: If you shake the meter too much, the lights will spike, so keep it as still as possible for accuracy. It's good practice to walk around the space you're in to check for natural electrical currents so that you don't confuse them with spirits once you start intentionally connecting with them. You may even find a ghost while you're checking the space! If you have looked around for outlets or wires with electric currents and have found none, place the EMF reader back where the original signal was coming from. If the signal is gone, that lends itself to a paranormal event. Or, if you place the EMF meter back and ask if something is standing there could it move a little to the side, and the lights fall based on your request, the device was likely connecting with a spirit.

TROUBLESHOOTING: The higher the frequency of the spirit, the harder it may be for them to use an EMF meter effectively. On a separate note, if a spirit has walked away, the meter may stop going off, even if you still feel their answers psychically. This is why you need to trust your intuition to know whether or not the spirit has moved or if the spirit is having difficulty gathering enough energy to use the meter.

Phasmabox

WHAT IT IS: Phasmabox is an audio-based application that allows the individual using it to more easily hear the spoken words of spirits. It is the only technology that has given me verifiable evidence of every kind of frequency and density of earth-based spirits. The app is advanced enough that I've even been able to carry on short conversations with entities while utilizing it. It is produced by eXtremeSenses, downloadable only for Windows computers. It's by far the easiest-to-use sound-based equipment I've ever tried. The app is relatively cheap, which makes it very accessible for most people. Phasmabox is dissimilar from phone apps in that it doesn't have a preset vocabulary bank, does not use any recording equipment, and does not require any Internet or cell reception. Personally, I have yet to find an application for cell phones that is as reliable as Phasmabox. The only downside is needing a PC, as Phasmabox has yet to make a cell phone app. The newest versions of the software include some visual elements, but I prefer the original version, which is purely sound-based and has no additional visual features besides the app controls themselves.

HOW TO USE IT: Once you've downloaded it, open up the program and move the toggle to On. Sounds may come through with additional echoes, unnaturally deep tones, and muffled whispers, all of which can sound unsettling to the newbie. It may take a little getting used to. I personally keep the Latin option off as well. (While the designers state that only English and Latin can come through, I've heard clear German, French, and other languages.) Above all, trust your intuition over any potential flare-ups from the Phasmabox. An off-sounding noise may not necessarily mean that a spirit is angry or that you are in any kind of spiritual danger.

KEEP IN MIND: This application can pick up on a wide variety of entities in a wide physical range. I've heard the spirits of two women bickering from a block away. You have to really pay attention to who is right by you and who is farther out. Spirits that are closer may sound louder or clearer than those farther out. Spirits who are farther away may not always be able to hear you, even if you pick up on them. It's similar to turning on an old open-channel walkie-talkie. In this case, instead of holding down a button to speak, you have to feel connected to the spirits you hear in some way to have them be able to properly pick up on you too. Connection can be as simple as calling out to them. You do not need to be near the Phasmabox application on your computer to have spirits hear you and to be heard speaking through the app. Utilize your psychic senses to do that. You can always ask other spirits to stop talking so that you can better hear the specific entity you're trying to talk to. You may also hear music associated with the place you're in or who you're speaking with. The Phasmabox is the only investigative tool that can accurately and distinctly pick up on different frequencies of spirits—even deities—so be aware that many kinds of entities might come through.

TROUBLESHOOTING: It can get a bit cumbersome lugging around a computer. I recommend bringing a bag. To hear properly, you may need a speaker or headphones. Ghosts love to drain lithium computer batteries as well, so you may need an extension cord or extra battery bank for the computer.

GENERAL TIPS FOR TECHNOLOGY

Using tech can be very exciting, and it can amp up the energy of everyone you're with, but be sure you don't get lost in all the noise and lights. Always remember to check in with yourself and your own balance. Excitement can be your friend, as long as it doesn't take over your wits. Loose emotions—even good ones—can sometimes create challenges for all involved when feelings go unchecked. Keep things light, but stay levelheaded.

Sometimes ghosts could care less about your tech validations. You may provide them snacks, drinks, books, and more, and still they don't care. For some spirits, being there is enough. Sometimes you picking up on them is all they care about, or maybe they don't even want you to pick up on them at all. Therefore, all you can do is try your best to get them to care. Otherwise, cut your losses, learn what you can from the experience, and move on.

GHOSTLY GO-TO

While the intentions of ghosts can vary from culture to culture, many ghost stories across the world maintain similar motifs, such as transparent figures, shadows, and passed loved ones presenting warnings to the living.

Your energy can also affect how well ghosts can respond to tech. Sometimes ghosts will use your excess energy to operate the tech. *Excess energy* refers to the energy that you release. For example, this can be as simple as the energy of a laugh: The laugh is out there, you are not exhausted by it, and you gave it willingly. In such circumstances you want to be sure that you're *sharing* excess energy rather than letting a spirit drain your energy—with or without you knowing it. If you feel the latter happening, remember to cleanse your energy and check your shield.

You may also come across a ghost who was expecting to use someone else's energy, is unable to do so, and as a result is unable to use the tech as it has in the past. Remember that fear is an excess energy source too. I do not offer spirits the energy of fear, which is why in some highly popularized haunted spaces the technical activity may be low with me. However, in speaking with the spirits and asking them about their previous experiences, I can sometimes read what those spirits have been able to do with tech in situations where others offered more loose energy than I choose to. Therefore, even if the tech isn't always spiking with me, I can at least quantify paranormal experiences from the past. This is yet another reason why trusting your psychic senses is so important when working with tech. It's not always about there being something wrong or off with you if devices aren't triggering as they have with others. Sometimes, especially if you go to paranormal places having little-to-no fear, the spirits may be more interested in talking rather than using their energy to perform.

Of course, let's not forget that sometimes your tech may not seem to "work" simply because a ghost may not like you. Maybe you look like someone that they hated long ago. Maybe they don't like your clothes. Maybe they just aren't in the mood to talk. Whatever the reason, no one feels like talking to everyone all the time. Sometimes it takes going back to a place time and time again to gain trust. Whatever the reason, just as you would do with the living, try not to take it personally, and move on.

For me, paranormal investigation always includes a psychic mediumship connection alongside understanding the technology I use. I always start by getting a feeling of where I ought to set up the equipment. If I'm well known at the location, I may have an easier time getting regular ghosts to talk to me, since that preestablished relationship is already present. The tech needs to be unintrusive and easily understood by a spirit from any time period. Understanding tech takes patience for anyone involved—those on the spiritual plane included. You can see some of these principles in action in the next story. It's from a time when one of the most haunted places in Wilmington graciously opened its doors to my spiritual curiosities.

GHOST STORY

WILMINGTON RAILROAD MUSEUM

Back in 1840, Wilmington, North Carolina, became the endpoint of the longest continuous railroad line in the world. It was called the Wilmington and Weldon Railroad and later known as the Atlantic Coast Line Railroad (ACL), and railroading was the lifeblood of Wilmington for over 125 years. In 1960 the city was shocked when ACL decided to move their headquarters to Jacksonville, Florida. The move left many warehouses and offices that had served freight and passenger lines empty and abandoned.

Where the Wilmington Railroad Museum sits today, there used to be eight lines of tracks. The museum itself is within a former warehouse, one of the only remaining buildings from the heyday of the rail line. As there are a plethora of spirits from the railroad days looking for places to go, the museum is a natural place for them to wind up. Within the warehouse-turned-museum there are many items the ghosts recognize, which helps them feel more at ease.

Having worked at this museum and later become part of its board of directors, I have run into many varieties of ghosts there, and they've taught me many things about life, death, and history. This museum was instrumental to my spiritual reawakening.

During the quiet off-season days when I worked behind the admissions desk, it was not uncommon for me to see various people out of the corner of my eye, or experience temperature anomalies, or hear footsteps when no one else was in the building. Once I became somewhat versed in paranormal investigation technology, the museum allowed me to go in after hours to get more quantifiable data on the spiritual activity that was going on within the building.

As the ghosts and I got to know each other over a long period of time, we were able to build up a positive rapport. While I was learning about the technological tools I wanted to use, I was able to teach the ghosts about them in real time. However, that's not to say that everybody was always receptive to what I wanted to do and when I wanted to do it.

I always explain to spirits that I want to work with them and learn from them. I tell them that I want people to become more interested in coming to the museum and learning about their history. Over time, the sounds of several ghosts have come through on the Phasmabox. (Supposedly, the Phasmabox can only produce words, but at the railroad museum I've heard it make the sounds of train horns and large bay doors groaning closed.) Additionally, through tech (and in the experiences of other employees I've talked with), big band music has been heard playing from speakers that no longer exist on our plane.

I've also set out touch lights in commonly used areas, such as in hallways and in front of bay doors. It's always exciting to see one light light up first, followed by one next to it and another next to that. It's a great way to see the speed at which a specter is walking. For the most part, the investigative tech has matched up very well with the psychic tools and intuition skills that I use. If anything, the biggest problem is figuring out who specifically I'm connecting with. There can be anywhere from three to fifteen people standing around during a given investigation.

One of the most fantastic pieces of evidence to date was caught on a livestream. I had just been talking with a man who zapped my computer battery. (Ghosts are prone to do this for their own energetic gains. Just as electrical currents can assist the physical body, it has been proven that electricity, including electricity from batteries, can also give ghosts a helpful energetic boost.) Fortunately, my phone—which was hosting the livestream—remained untouched by spirits throughout the night. As I filmed, other psychically inclined people were reading in to that same ghost. The ghost admitted to them, through dowsing rods—a psychic tool I'll go into detail about later—to having drained the computer battery. This allowed viewers and me to cross-validate what we were sensing. Then, unexpectedly, the window just in front of me started shaking as if a train had roared by. Immediately after that, I heard footsteps on the roof. Lastly, there were a few clicking sounds from something on the opposite side of the room.

After the event, I searched the area to see if there was anything that would've made the experiences physically explainable. Having spent time in the museum for years, I knew I had never heard anything like that happen to the windows. There was nothing nearby that could've picked up that kind of speed to move the air around it. No one was walking on the boardwalk just outside the window, either. And if it had been wind, the other windows would have shaken as well.

What's more, hearing only a few footsteps on the roof didn't make any logical sense. How would someone have gotten on the roof in the first place? Where did they go after walking only a few steps? And lastly, where did the strange clicking noises come from?

This museum is still one of my favorite places to visit, both for community and for spiritual activity. I regularly encourage people to go and see it for themselves, especially during the quiet season. As for catching the paranormal activity, after the successes I've had in the past, they now offer public reservation options to rent the museum for paranormal investigations.

PSYCHIC TOOLS

Personally, I gravitate toward psychic tools over paranormal investigation tools. For me, psychic tools have always been immediately effective. They require no electricity, batteries, or special skills beyond spiritual connection. And psychic tools can be used *with* investigative tools for further validation. Here are some common psychic tools:

Dowsing Rods

WHAT THEY ARE: A pair of *L*-shaped rods that you hold on to by grasping their shorter sides. These rods have been used for thousands of years to find underground water reserves. The rods will cross like an *X* for a yes and move away from each other for a no. *Maybe* is the interpretation when one rod moves out and the other remains straight.

HOW TO USE THEM: Hold the handles so that the rods point straight in front of you. Try to create as even an area as possible between the rods in your hands so that the rods don't move around from the sway of your body or the natural movement of your hands. The rods should run parallel to the ground and point straight in front of you at the beginning. Relax your thumbs over your fingers. Steady yourself. Ask the rods to cross for a yes. You can also use the rods to find things (like ghosts) for you. The rods will point toward what you're looking for. I recommend trying this out at home with fun, low-pressure searches and questions before going to a haunted spot.

KEEP IN MIND: Use the rods for yourself first. Ask to see a yes to a question you already know the answer to so that you can practice. Practice using the rods to find lost items around your house. Ask them where your pet is and see how they move. If the rods point to a seemingly empty corner, check in with your psychic skills. A passed pet may be hanging out with you!

TROUBLESHOOTING: If you question yourself too much, the rods won't work for you. Relax. Get into the daydreamy state. The rods may only move a little for you at first. Their movement will only be as strong as your connection to yourself and to whoever you're looking to talk to.

GHOSTLY GO-TO

Cave paintings in North Africa may depict civilizations utilizing dowsing rods as far back as 8,000 years ago! The rods are most commonly used for finding minerals and underground water sources for wells.

Oracle Cards

WHAT THEY ARE: There are many different types of oracle cards. They can be similar to tarot cards, but they often lack the tradition of rules and restrictions that comes along with tarot. With oracle cards, you can look at the image provided on the card, allow your eye to be drawn to an aspect of that image, and utilize what it's trying to tell you from there. If tarot cards are your preference, you are welcome to use them; I prefer oracle cards, especially for beginners, since they present a smaller learning curve.

HOW TO USE THEM: It's good practice to cleanse your cards before and after each use. You can use any of the techniques for cleansing described in this book. Some people like to shuffle their cards and allow specific cards to fall out. Some like to pull a card at random from the stack.

KEEP IN MIND: Cards are best used for discovering the emotions and feelings of ghosts. This means you can use them to help you cross-validate your clairtangency. Reading your cards will allow you to better understand why a spirit is feeling a particular way. Some people like to ask for yes and no responses based on even- and odd-numbered cards.

TROUBLESHOOTING: Trusting that the right card will come out is essential. Overthinking which card to pick will keep you from getting a straight answer.

I recommend practicing reading the cards while connecting with your own energy first, before using them with another's energy (incarnate or not).

Pendulum

WHAT IT IS: A light weight at the end of a chain or string. A pendulum can be as fancy or simple as you like; for example, I've used a ring on a shoelace before. You could even use a necklace. As long as you have a weight at the end of a cord, you have a pendulum.

HOW TO USE IT: Keep your arm as still as possible—either tuck your elbow in and extend your hand out, or rest your elbow on a flat surface—and hold the string or cord out, letting the pendulum hang. Ask the pendulum to move in a circular or back-and-forth motion. Be sure your arm and hand stay as still as possible.

KEEP IN MIND: As with the dowsing rods, you'll want to practice working with a pendulum on your own and with your own energy first. Some people like to use a pendulum board with *yes*, *no*, *maybe*, and other words written out. I prefer to ask my pendulum to move in a circle for yes and back and forth for no. Some people like to have their pendulum move clockwise for yes and counterclockwise for no. Figure out what works best for you.

TROUBLESHOOTING: Make working with a pendulum fun. You can ask it to swing in different directions to help you find things. Let it feel like a game. Yes, you want your interpretations to be true; however, if you're too caught up in that desperation, the tool will be affected. Relax. Keep it fun.

Flame / Smoke

WHAT IT IS: Flames and smoke can be used for scrying—that is, seeing and interpreting images in everyday things. This can be a spiritual activity as well as a form of psychic perception—specifically clairvoyance. If you've ever looked at clouds and seen pictures, and those pictures acted as a metaphor for something you were going through, you've scried.

HOW TO USE IT: Looking into fire or smoke, allow your eyes to relax. Lose yourself in the light of the flames or the waves of the smoke. Ask yourself a question. See what image the smoke or flame and your mind lead you to. Then ask yourself, *What does it mean?* Spirits can use smoke and fire too. Fire is energy. Ghosts and other spiritual beings can sometimes make the flame of a candle burn tall and straight for yes or low and dull for no. Sometimes they can manipulate the smoke to flow in a particular direction.

KEEP IN MIND: Whether working with your own perception or with a spirit, practice is key. You also want to be sure that you're being safe and have permission to have a candle or flame. The caretakers of a historic site will likely not allow you to do this. However, while camping or at your home, you can try this as long as you feel safe doing so. If flame is not your preference, you can light an incense stick to create smoke.

TROUBLESHOOTING: Flames can often encourage you to look inward. If you find that doing this activity leads you to understand yourself more than it helps you to perceive outward, that's okay! Take it for what it is and enjoy learning the lessons along the way.

GENERAL TIPS FOR ALL TOOLS

All tools are useful if they allow you to feel psychically validated while also providing verifiable evidence that can be supported historically. As you're starting out, tools may help you to trust yourself more by understanding when you're right or wrong regarding whatever it is you are perceiving. It's important to try out a variety of tools so you can discover what works best for your growth.

Make Your Own Way

Is there a tool you want to try using that this chapter didn't mention? Go for it! This is intuition, after all—follow the path that you feel most led to go down. Years ago I felt so overwhelmed with what everyone else was doing that I let it shut down part of my self-trust and development. Then, when I let myself take the route of curiosity, I began to collect rocks. I used the rocks as metaphors to help me better understand psychic information. No one told me how to do this; I just found it fun. After some practice, I've found validations in my readings. Years later, I learned this was something like the ancient practice of lithiomancy (using stones and the light reflecting off stones to predict the future). How amazing it felt to have intuitively found a way of reading spiritual energy, only to find others had been using something similar across space and time!

GHOSTLY GO-TO

Recent psychological research has found that how you feel about a new skill is just as important as the skill itself. When learning, it's important to incorporate curious playtime into your routine to entice yourself into the experience and see it as fun, refreshing, and useful for your brain.

Having said that, it's also important to never get stuck in only one form of reading or technology. Always stay open-minded about what you want to know and how you want to get that information. You may find a way that works great for you most of the time but then decide that for some communication you prefer a different tool or practice. The point of all of this is for you to know that you have options to help you find validation in your psychic reads.

Checking Your Connections

Sometimes tech will pick up and connect with one spirit while your psychic tools will connect with another. From experience, I can tell you this can really be a disappointment when you're trying to trust your psychic senses. While tech is harder to control when it comes to what it's connecting with, psychic tools can get more specific. If the answers through the tech are different from the ones you're getting using psychic tools, ask your tools if they're connecting with the same being. Here are some ideas on ways to use both kinds of tools to find out more about who you're connecting with:

- You can use dowsing rods or flashlights to ask yes and no questions.
- A Phasmabox can be used to ask if whoever you're speaking to likes music or can play an instrument.
- Oracle cards may be used to receive better information on what spirits are going through emotionally.
- EMF readers can be used both to find ghosts around you and to have them answer questions—different levels of excitement will determine how far the lights light up.

Get creative with how you use your tools! You may never know if a ghost prefers one kind of tool over another until you give them some options about which tools to use for what.

Also, you may be connected to the same being with both your tech and psychic tools, but sometimes ghosts lie. I had an experience in the Savannah Paranormal Museum where a being was being picked up on through both tech and my dowsing rods. Most of the answers it gave through tech lined up perfectly with those I received with the dowsing rods, except for a specific few. How did I know to trust my rods over the tech? Practice. I trust my rods, because they're connected to the trust I have in my own energy and ability. I know that when I connect to a being through my dowsing rods, I connect to their truth.

Checking Your Bias

If you're worried that your answers may be lining up too much with your own energy rather than the energy of who you're working with, you can navigate around this with the help of a trusted friend. For any of the psychic tools mentioned, you can, with your friend's permission, connect with *their* energy to practice finding answers. Have them write down a numbered list of ten questions. Once they've written down the questions and know the answers for themself, use your tools to discover what their answers are. If an answer to one of the questions doesn't come to you immediately, skip that one and continue.

Once done, compare your answers with theirs. If you needed to skip a question, talk about what you felt and ask your friend what they felt about their answer. Learn for yourself why it was difficult for you to figure out an answer. Sometimes the energy of a *maybe* can feel confused. That doesn't mean you're a bad reader; you're merely learning how you understand the psychic information you're getting.

To this day, if I'm ever feeling like my psychic energy is off, I will ask my partner to play psychic games with me. Sometimes I'll ask them to think of a color, number, or situation. Other times I'll ask them to think about something that happened the day before. I trust my senses and use tools as needed. If I'm off in my perception, I know I need to clarify my connections before doing any readings for others that day—by recleansing my energy, grounding, and shielding.

PSYCHIC TOOLS DEBATE

Be prepared, because some people, no matter how impressive your results may be, will never believe in the psychic tools you use. Some paranormal investigators will only ever swear by specific tech and will never allow any other mode of communication to have a say. In any situation, it's up to you either to believe in the validation you found and that it can be replicated, or to try something else. Use your tools for your own validation. It's not about anyone else, and you'll strengthen your self-trust and psychic skills as a result. The reality is, as long as your means are ethical and respectful, it shouldn't matter how you get your ghostly evidence, as long as it's based in truth.

GHOSTLY GO-TO

Mesopotamian texts contain some of the earliest records of ghosts appearing. Ancient Greek and Roman texts, including historical as well as fictional writing, also describe interactions with ghosts.

IN SUMMARY

Whether they rely on new technology or on ancient psychic practices, tools can assist you in trusting in your intuition. They can serve as excellent supports to help you feel that your psychic mediumship is real. While these are great aids, I implore you to only use them as just that: aids. They are not the root of your psychic ability. Always utilize your psychic skills first, and use tools to help you better understand the information you're receiving.

HERE ARE SOME KEY POINTS TO REMEMBER:

- Make your psychic mediumship reads before pulling out tech and tools.
- Ghosts don't all know how to use tech. Sometimes you will need to work with them to help them understand it.
- Your energy can affect how well ghosts are able to use tech. Pivot as needed.
- Make your own way! It's okay to create new techniques and reading styles, as long as your methods give you straightforward, truthful information.
- Always check your bias, and check that your various tools are connecting with the same ghost at the same time.

CHAPTER 8

EXPLORING AND SHARING YOUR ENCOUNTERS

The previous chapters have set you up with all you need to have excellent (and safe) encounters with the incorporeal world. In this chapter you'll discover what it means to trust your intuition about where to go, who to connect with, and for how long. You'll see that everyone experiences an occasional bump in the road when exploring their psychic senses, and that there's no shame in getting something wrong. You'll learn even more ways to validate your psychic reads through researching your encounters, and you'll explore how to share your stories with others, both online and face to face.

TRUST YOUR SENSES

My favorite kind of ghost encounter is when I meet an individual to whom I truly feel intuition has connected me. Sometimes it can be easy to get caught up in finding a specific spirit that you've heard about, but often in doing that you miss the signs and begin to doubt your abilities. Instead, trust that in every place you go, there's something for you to find. Humans are natural scavengers and finders of things, so why not follow that same inclination with your intuition? You know spirits are out there, and you may not know which one you'll find, but you need to trust that you will find the right one for you.

For every historically famous ghost I've met, I've come across at least twenty to thirty ghosts who fell through the cracks between easier-to-find documented figures. Because of this, sometimes when I happen to find myself with a ghost who is infamous, it takes me a while to accept that they're actually well known. To check my connections, I set up all kinds of psychic checkpoints for myself, just to ensure that who I'm talking to is who they say they are. I have trained myself to consider the reality that most spirits were never famous. That way, when I do become convinced I'm talking with someone whose story has withstood the test of time, I can trust the information I'm receiving.

GHOST STORY

BLACKBEARD'S GHOST

I met Blackbeard. Yes, the Blackbeard. Famed privateer. The most famous name to come out of the golden age of piracy. That Blackbeard. His ghost has reportedly been seen up and down the East Coast and in just about every southeastern port city that dates from the colonial era. Cities from Savannah, Georgia, to Charleston, South Carolina, claim to have the ghost of the legendary Blackbeard. I happened to meet him in the small town of Bath, North Carolina.

The town of Bath was the first officially incorporated city in the colony of North Carolina. It sits on a quiet creek that gently empties into Pamlico Sound. Bath was where the famed Edward Teach resided after he was pardoned by the king for his first stint as a pirate. Of course, if you know the history, you know it wasn't long after that event that Teach decided piracy was the best way to suit his needs, and he went right back to it.

Blackbeard lived and pillaged in various places up and down the American East Coast. It makes sense that he, in different iterations, could haunt any of these places. What I wasn't expecting, though, was to find him in such a quiet place. History often forgets that this man lived a relatively quiet life for most of his years. It was only in the last few years of his life that he pursued piracy—and it's those last few years that made him infamous.

When I visited Bath, I had no idea that Blackbeard had once lived there or that there were ghost stories surrounding his time there. What I originally intended to be a quiet weekend with Tharyn turned into a pretty adventurous ghost search. It started very simply. Just after dark, when almost all the town had closed for the evening, the two of us went out with a phone, our Phasmabox, and our intuition. We asked the ghosts in town, who were not hard to find even from the street, if they knew where any spirits of pirates were. We were surprised that not only did they confirm that ghost pirates were in town, but they also went so far as to say that Blackbeard was still around.

While the living seem to be fascinated with piracy, the ghosts were anything but. While they confirmed that pirate ghosts were nearby, they were uninterested in talking about Blackbeard or privateers. They even had some colorfully derogatory words to call Blackbeard, which we recorded. When we asked if they knew where his ghost was, they gave a few different answers. This meant that we each had to trust our intuition in deciding which advice to follow. Tharyn was led in one direction, whereas I was led the opposite way, and a third direction also seemed possible.

We later learned that all three tips were correct. Tharyn had been led in the direction of Teach's Cove. This was a location where Blackbeard was said to have hidden out while he was waiting for the king's pardon. However, at the time, Tharyn had no idea that's where they were standing. There were no markers. It was only after a web search that we had any idea of what was suspected to have happened in that area.

I was led in the direction of what we later found out was Blackbeard's residence. At the place I was led to, there's a historical marker talking about Blackbeard having lived in town. The structure itself was likely across the sound in an area we didn't have access to. We were later able to confirm that with a historian.

The third direction, which both of us picked up on, seemed a little bit too on the nose. We were told Blackbeard was by the waterfront. I kept getting an image in my mind of a man sitting on the dock and fishing. It seemed so simple. Was that really Edward Teach? The image felt too specific for me to have made it up on the spot. I felt as if one of the nearby ghosts had shared it with me. However, knowing of no public access to the waterfront, we decided to pack up for the night.

At different junctures, each of us had seen a large outline of a figure who appeared to be fishing from a pier. So, the next day, we made our way to a public pier owned by the local historic site. It was there that our intuition proved to be correct. While out on the pier, we positioned ourselves near where we saw the figure fishing, then we set up our Phasmabox and asked again where Blackbeard was. From far off, we could hear a ghost calling him offensive names from the shoreline. Occasionally, a loud, low grumble came from close proximity to where

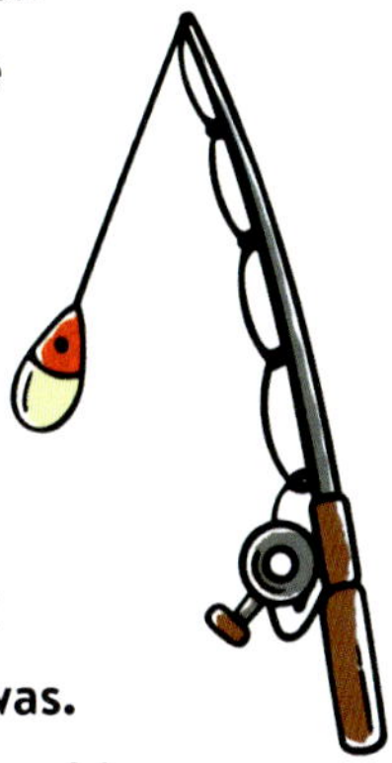

we were, but besides that, the man we sat next to was uninterested in proving his existence to us.

His silence held until we asked if we could pay him to provide some kind of validation for us. After we asked how we could pay him, I had a vision of gold coins in my head and Tharyn heard the word *gold.* We got out what coins we had and left them close to him, and he seemed pleased enough. It wasn't immediate, and it certainly wasn't enthusiastic, but eventually, between the ghost shouting from the shoreline and the quiet fisherman sitting next to us, we got a name not once but twice: Edward.

I think many people would expect someone like Blackbeard to be found in a rambunctious place similar to the ones he frequented in his most famous stories. Few would expect to find him having more of a connection to the simpler parts of his life. Apparently, he enjoyed the quiet, relaxing activity of fishing. While we were with him, we could even feel a small jolt of excitement whenever a fish jumped out of the water. He eyed the fish like a predator on the hunt. His energy was like that of a volcano—calm on the surface, but with moving lava beneath.

I didn't go looking for a famous pirate. Even as more clues came through our cross-validated psychic-trained minds in addition to the investigative tech, my first instinct was to believe it wasn't true. Could a last-minute venture to a sleepy colonial town really lead to meeting one of the biggest figures in privateer history? In my case, yes. However, I did not go into the experience expecting to find the famous man we eventually found. I

believe that all I can do is trust the intuitive process. If fate is meant to work in such a way that the path of an ordinary person like myself crosses the path of someone infamous, then let it.

THREE KEY WAYS TO VALIDATE YOUR READS

The following methods for validating your reads are not in any particular, required order, but ideally you'll be looking to use all three in any given situation. Sometimes you'll be able to validate a psychic read in all three ways. In the event you do, be sure to celebrate your moment of accomplishment! However, if you don't, note the experience, learn anything you can from it, and trust that if you're meant to find validation, it will come to you when it's meant to come to you.

Investigative Tech Check

Whenever possible, always do your psychic reads before you pull out any investigative tech. You can always keep your psychic abilities tuned in once the tech comes on—and I recommend you do just that—but whenever possible, let the tech wait until you've read everything you can. While you *can* do it the other way around (start with tech and then lean into intuition), you will feel far more validated if you read first and then check your reads with tech. Ideally, you will be able to hear or see information through tech that *adds* to what you perceive through your skills.

If you happen to be with a group of people who want to use tech right away and don't want to wait for you to read, do what you can to temporarily distance yourself from them to avoid distraction. This may mean creating an energetic shield that's specifically and temporarily between you and those with the tech. It may even mean leaving the room that they're in and doing a little investigation on your own if you feel comfortable doing so. You can always join back up with the group later. It's even possible that the ghosts you're connecting with will talk, through the tech, about your reads.

GHOSTLY GO-TO

Checking psychic mediumship reads with technology is a relatively new option. Before the invention of controlled electricity and audio recording devices, divination tools and memory were the only ways to fact-check a medium on the spot.

Psychic Medium Check

If you're in a place where you feel a ghost and you happen to be with someone who also considers themself spiritually sensitive, check in with each other! To ensure that you're both doing your due diligence in reading, you should temporarily separate and spend time in specific spots where you feel spiritual activity. Individually focus in on those spots and the spirits in them. It could be two different corners of the same room or different areas of a building. Write down anything you perceive. Remember to make your notes as detailed as possible. When you're both ready, switch spots and repeat the process. Then share your answers with each other. This approach allows each of you to do your best on your own. If your answers differ, you must decide what you want to believe—this is no reason for a fight. You can always use tech, history, or another spiritually sensitive person to break the tie later.

GHOSTLY GO-TO

You may also book time with a professional to go over reads with you. If you do, make sure that the psychic medium you're looking to book with can read ghosts. Even if you're not at the haunted site any longer, some psychic mediums can still read the energy and let you know what they pick up on—so we may be able to help. Of course, do your research before making a booking.

History Check

New historical information is always being uncovered. Keep that in mind as you search for documentation of whoever you connect with on the other side. There are many directions you can look in to learn more about history, whether it's reading a nearby historical marker, doing a web search, visiting the local section of a library, or asking a historian. In some places, there are even active archaeological digs that the public can witness and interact with.

While specific names may be hard to find in a historical search, general information about time periods, major events, and day-to-day life may be better documented. The most satisfying kind of validation happens when you go into a place whose history you know nothing about and meet a spirit that reveals some part of that history to you, and then, through research, you're able to discover that the information gathered from the spirit world is in fact true. Look to be surprised. Stay curious and open-minded. Always ask questions and trust you'll be led where you need to go.

GHOST STORY

THE SAME GHOST

When I meet with clients who want me to make connections with the ghosts where they are, I prefer to learn as little as possible from the client before the session. This allows me to follow whatever energy feels strongest. I read the energy and report back what I find. The best feeling is seeing the look of shock and recognition on a client's face when I present the details from my blind read. Not only am I able to feel further confidence in my psychic ability, but they too are able to feel like trusting their intuition was the right choice to make. The best kind of verified cross-validation is when two or more people who do not know anything about each other or the space that they're in can have the same spiritual experience. Here's an example.

The client I was meeting with told me that she thought she was seeing a ghost, but she had no other proof of what was going on. No one else in her home considered themself spiritually sensitive, and neither the house nor the land it was on had an obvious history that would sug-

gest haunting. Each experience only gave her more questions. One day, she saw my videos online and decided to take a chance and make an online booking.

Once she had told me I was looking for a ghost, I kindly asked her not to disclose any further information. I asked if I had her permission to energetically look for this ghost around her house. She consented, and I was off.

First, I encountered the typical energies one might find in a house with a family. Different rooms were associated with different feelings based on the activities that happened within them. Some old family heirlooms had bits of residual energy from passed loved ones who were not there at the time. I kept searching for a low-frequency energy until I found a very clear one just outside her back door.

I began to describe to her who I was picking up on. He was a white, bearded man. He had deep wrinkles on his face from the sun, but he didn't feel older than thirty-five. His hair was dark, and so were his eyes. He had a naturally lean build with some muscles from his work. He struck me as a kind of lumberjack, with his button-up red flannel shirt loosely tucked in to sturdy, tried-and-true blue jeans. His boots were large, leather, and worn.

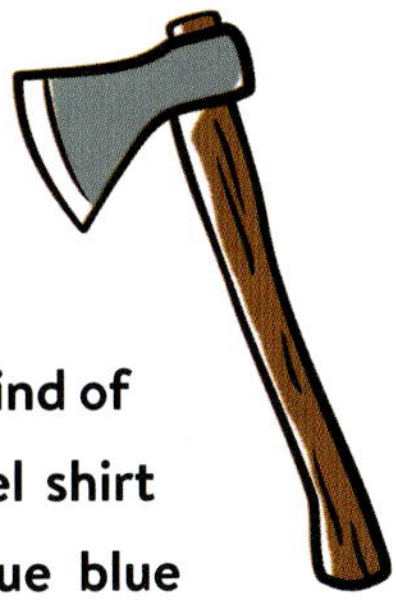

After describing the man, I refocused my vision back to the woman. She had tears in her eyes, but her face was otherwise blank. "That's the exact man I've seen," she said.

I asked her if she was all right, and she laughed a little and wiped away a tear. "I thought I was losing my mind, but how could you have known what I never told you?"

"I guess that makes me psychic," I joked.

We talked through some of the other details of the man. She seemed relieved and began to open up more about her experiences. Once I began to speak with the man, I discovered that he had lived in a small, nearby cabin that had long since fallen away to time. He had worked as a lumberman around the area. One day, he woke up, saw that his house was gone, and happened to see a new, larger home nearby. He was drawn to the energy inside and took to sitting out on the back porch. The client confirmed that the area she lived in had been a site of logging activity fifty or so years prior to her moving there.

The consultation ended with me bridging the conversation gap between the two of them by providing some tips on how they could speak with each other more. While he wasn't a talkative man, he seemed pleased to have her company from time to time. When she booked her follow-up meeting with me—something I offer to ensure that whatever was done in the initial conversation is still meeting everyone's needs—she excitedly told me of how things were progressing. I was just as ecstatic to hear more about the newfound trust she was able to have in herself.

HOW TO RESEARCH YOUR ENCOUNTER

After you have had an encounter with a ghost, it's important to research as much as possible about the area you are in and its history to help validate your read. The point of a theory is to test it to see if it truly holds up. Once you've had a spiritual encounter, see if the historical details you encountered make sense through the context of someone else's knowledge and experience. Here are some first steps toward finding out about where you are and what may have happened there:

- If no one is close by who can answer your questions about the specific location, take photos. Typically, a few photos will be enough to help you describe the setting to a knowledgeable person later.
- If you're outside or in a spot that may be difficult to describe later, open up a map application on your phone, zoom out a little, and take a screenshot.
- Do a quick search to see if there are any nearby roadside historical signs. Oftentimes these signs are placed in popular areas rather than right on top of where an important event occurred.

Once you've documented all that you can from the site itself, start your research. If you can stay in the nearby area, see if there are any museums you can visit. If the museum doesn't have information on the time period you're looking for, ask someone to refer you to where you can learn more. This may lead you to a library or to a local who knows how the area has changed over time. Sometimes the best way to find information is the same way you found a ghost: Trust yourself and start talking to people!

Internet searches can also assist you in finding what you're looking for. However, in a time of AI and algorithms there are a few stipulations regarding web searches. If you can, use an incognito browser that is not connected to the specific location of your IP address. This will provide you with a more open search. Also, do not rely on AI to compile material for your web research; click on links and read the material for yourself.

GHOSTLY GO-TO

Intuitive web searches are another way to research. Let your eyes be drawn to the links and pictures you ought to visit. Let your feelings dictate whether or not to keep looking where you're looking. Be sure to stay grounded and level-headed in your search, as the feeling of desperation is not a productive one. Get into the daydreamy theta state and let yourself be led to where you need to go.

Be sure that your research on your encounter is as thorough and unbiased as possible. When doing web searches, look for citations from professionally reviewed sources. Rather than being overly specific in your search terms, leave your questions open-ended. For example, *Was there a mill on top of where the soccer field is now?* is a leading question. Try something more open, such as *What was here before the soccer field was here?* City maps from different decades may be helpful. So may conversations with people who have lived in the area a long time and know about the history of the location.

To this day, I don't always have all the answers as to why each ghost is in the spot they're found in. There is no one-size-fits-all scenario. What I do know is that sometimes it doesn't matter how much things may have changed on the outside; the inside of a ghost's mind may continue to show a picture from the past that has long since fallen away. Even in the times when I'm unsure what to believe when a ghost tells me their story, I've found that if I'm meant to know the truth, with a bit of initiative, the information will come my way. Little did I know that a ghost would reveal an entire lost building to me one night at a present-day bar in Wilmington.

GHOST STORY

"NO ONE KNOWS I DIED HERE"

Before I knew I was clairvoyant, let alone a psychic medium, I suddenly and in vivid detail saw how a man had been murdered. I was tired and a little cold and had just gone into Cape Fear Wine & Beer after having hosted a ghost tour. Having spent my energy providing a solid performance, I slumped up to the bar, ordered a cider, and sat down at an empty table to wait for two of my friends.

Unknowingly, I was already well into a daydreamy state. I hadn't even gotten to sip my cider when I thought I saw a shadow out of the corner of my eye. The shadow passed to my side. The hair on my arm started to stand up. Before I could register that it was a ghost, I saw a

vision. I knew it wasn't *my* vision, because it had never happened to me. It felt like a dream I had been placed in.

I was in a back room. Muffled sounds of jazz and the commotion that comes with a crowded bar could be heard outside the room. I was on my knees. I could tell I was wearing a suit by the way my body felt. My hands were clutching my pants. Cold sweat dripped down the sides of my brow. I knew a man stood behind me to block a door—my only way out. Another man stood in the corner. A third man was before me. All were wearing nice suits and had slicked-back hair. The man before me held the nose of a gun to my face.

Bam.

I was back at the bar. I could feel my eyes were wide, but I wasn't afraid. The feeling of desperation from only a second ago had vanished. I could feel the energy of the shadow behind me. Without thinking about it, I asked him through my mind, "Was that you?"

"I died here," he said sadly. He then gave me his name and his age. "No one knows I died here."

I nodded, "I know."

"Thank you," he said.

The feeling of the shadow dissipated as I saw him move out from behind me and into nothing. My friends showed up soon after. They were already talking about an annoying customer they had met while they were waiting tables earlier in the night. I gulped, pushed the experience down, and joined the waking world again.

While I assumed that the bar I was in had not always been a bar, the picture in my vision hadn't matched the current interior at all. I'd seen a nicer-looking parlor or back room. I felt like I had seen mob members. Was the mob in Wilmington? And what was the room I saw? It had warm lights, rich pastel colors, and crown molding all around. It felt like a bustling hotel with a party going on just outside the door.

Six months after the experience, I found myself back at Cape Fear Wine & Beer with another group of friends. As fate would have it, one of them knew the history of the building. He told me that where we sat used to be the lobby of an old hotel. While the first floor and basement of the hotel remained, the top five floors had burned down decades before. He then told me that the hotel had connections to the mob during prohibition.

I could have cried! By that point I had convinced myself I'd made the encounter with the man up in my mind. It had made no sense until then! Feeling emboldened, I told my friends about the experience I'd had months before. I was grateful to find they were ghost enthusiasts who had their own experiences to share from the same bar!

DEALING WITH "FAILURE": WHAT IF YOU'RE WRONG?

So what if you're wrong? It happens to us all. For example, if there's one aspect of psychic mediumship that I am not 100 percent accurate on, it is names. I can be standing next to another verified psychic and get nine specified attributes about a ghost's character, presence, and appearance spot-on. But if the grand finale is getting the name of the ghost, well, I wish myself good luck. In all my years of experience, I will say I have a 60 percent chance of getting a name entirely correct. Does that make me any less a psychic medium? No. One wrong answer next to nine correct ones creates a 90 percent rate of reading accuracy overall. How many people do you know in your everyday life who can maintain such a high rate of correctness in their job?

Early on as a psychic medium, I suffered from imposter syndrome. I would have astonishing sessions with people. I would know things time after time. And then I would get one thing wrong and totally implode. Sometimes I would have a consultation with someone, get something incorrect, and afterward break down in tears. I didn't want to let anyone down, and I put such high expectations on myself that it caused me a lot of anxiety. Some days I wouldn't take appointments because I got so lost in the *What if I'm wrong?* mentality.

Why did I struggle with this? Because none of the resources I found for psychic development ever referenced the reality that *failure happens*. Being "wrong" merely means that you need to reassess. While embracing intuition doesn't need to be complicated, understanding the intricacies of how you perceive information can sometimes feel complex. Sometimes you throw your perception out so wide that you pick up on someone two buildings over rather than the ghost standing right next to you. Sometimes a ghost wants nothing to do with you but everything to do with a different person. Sometimes you pick up on a very masculine presence that happens to be from a woman. Give yourself some grace. Be kind to yourself and others. Apologize when you need to. As long as you are genuine, many spirits will be forgiving, as long as they really want to talk.

If someone is going to throw out the validity of your entire reading based on one answer being wrong, you were never going to convince that person of anything anyway. People will either believe or they won't. Your job isn't to try and force them into your belief system. Your responsibility is to be true to yourself.

SHARING YOUR EXPERIENCES

Talking about ghosts will make many people uncomfortable. For some people, it goes against their religious beliefs, as ghosts create questions that they're not ready to explore for themselves. Other people are afraid enough of the dark as it is and don't want to even think about what unseen things could be there. The philosophical folks may fall down the rabbit hole of *Why are there ghosts to begin with?*, leading to a reflective pool that not everyone is ready to look into. Whatever their reason for trepidation, the point is, you can't make anyone believe you. *You* must believe you. Your belief must begin and end with you.

Often, a person sees a ghost and then needs everyone else to believe them. While, yes, we all want to be believed, you can't convince someone to believe in the afterlife and ghosts if they don't want to. You must make peace with yourself. Sometimes, saying "I don't know what I saw, but I know I saw something" is confidence enough.

GHOSTLY GO-TO

No one should expect you to have all the answers. They may want more details about your spiritual experience, but that doesn't mean you should be expected to have a detailed answer to every question about what you experienced. If you ever feel like someone is belittling you, cut your losses on the topic and move on to something else.

The hard reality is, not everyone believes in ghosts, ghost stories, or the idea that anyone can connect with ghosts. As much as I wish I could tell you that my Internet and in-person experiences telling my stories have been entirely positive, that would not be true. What I know for myself is that my abilities do not harm me or anyone else. People may choose to listen or not, and that is entirely up to them. The point is that having these experiences means something to me, and that is why I keep sharing them.

GHOST STORY

GHOST WALKS

I consider myself very fortunate to live in a relatively small and highly walkable city. It's not that I'm constantly on the lookout for ghosts; I enjoy walking around to clear my mind and get my blood going. Walking is an easy way to slip into that daydreamy state. Oftentimes, I'm very open to interacting with ghosts. However, there have been plenty of occasions where I want to listen to music and be in my own thoughts. This is why I have a variety of different shields for different occasions.

At the times I do want to meet ghosts, I ask myself questions on my walks, such as, *Is anyone nearby?* Sometimes I'll just know a spirit is there through claircognizance. Other times, I send out a kind of cloud that silently moves around ghosts like a sonar system. Every now and then I get the inner-ear clairaudience feeling that someone just said "Hey" or called my name.

As I walk, I allow myself to meander in whatever direction I feel a pull toward. I pay attention to a light tug or pull that comes from my chest. I never know what I'm looking for most of the time, but as long as the feeling is safe and interesting, I follow it. At any point, I can always turn around and backtrack. Feelings change. It doesn't suddenly mean I've

lost my intuition. Action and the future are still mutable, after all. The point is that sometimes I don't care to stick around and find out why the feeling changed. I trust myself enough to acknowledge the change and switch my direction.

To this day I have regular encounters that I can't often explain. Sometimes spirits move around and it's impossible to know where they came from. Many ghosts in a haunted place like Wilmington are doing their own things. They don't need to be messed with. They don't have time for questions. Other times, I speak with spirits. They'll tell me what they're doing. Some are even a little starstruck if they've heard of me. Wilmington has a thriving ghost gossip network! Even when they do open up about who they remember themselves to be and where they came from, I don't always have the evidence to prove the reality of the interaction to anyone. I don't walk with paranormal investigative tech on me. I usually don't have a historical interpreter standing with me. At best, I have my notes application to jot down the conversation. Even then, some interactions are so fleeting that only my memory can log them at all.

Even as I write this, I consider the reality that you may not believe everything I've told you and every interaction I've had. That's okay. My true hope is that you have the same peace in your beliefs that I do, whatever those beliefs may be.

CONNECTING WITH THE LARGER PARANORMAL COMMUNITY

There are many online forums you can visit where you can find a sea of people who believe in ghosts and are looking for further proof of the paranormal. However, at some point, you'll need to decide what your expectations are when it comes to what kind of community you're looking for.

This is where your intuition can serve you in your everyday life. When you're searching for groups and people to talk to, get specific with yourself about what you're looking for. Are you looking for friends? Confirmations? People to challenge you? Skeptics? Spiritualists? Once you've decided what you're looking for—which can change in the future as needed—ask yourself, *Is this the place I want to put my energy?*

GHOSTLY GO-TO

According to a YouGov poll from 2022, around two-thirds of Americans believe they have had what they consider a paranormal experience. Women are more likely than men to report their experiences and believe psychic abilities are possible.

When considering a certain community or group, look at how it's run. Notice:

- Is every experience always interpreted to involve a ghost?
- Is no encounter ever interpreted to involve a ghost?
- Are constructive questions being asked?
- Are members encouraged to think and be considerate before typing up a post or response?
- What kinds of rules do they have?
- Do they moderate their posts, and who is leading the discussions?

For me, the most important quality is thoughtfulness. Of course, not all groups can be monitored 24/7, but in the long term, threads and posts need to have some constructive structure. If you feel some aspect of the group isn't aligned with you from the beginning, remember that it is up to you whether or not you choose to stay. There are plenty of trolls who choose to spend their time belittling people who believe in ghosts, even in paranormal groups.

There are also clear differences between someone trying to bully you based on your experiences and someone who is asking questions to understand and gather quantifiable data. Not everyone who challenges you is trying to insult you. Know what you're willing to put up with. It can feel deeply personal to be questioned when you're already not sure of what you feel or believe. Remember that, at some point, you will need to shrug off others' beliefs and feelings and decide whether or not what you've experienced and believe is authentic to you.

IN SUMMARY

The value of the experience you get out of communicating with the other side will always come down to you. The energy that you put into your encounters—both before and after they happen—will have a direct effect on how much you'll want to continue to pursue trusting your intuition.

HERE ARE SOME KEY POINTS TO REMEMBER:

- Trust your senses and enjoy the journey.
- You can check your mediumship through investigative tech, through a psychic medium, and through historical research.
- Be sure your historical research about your encounter is as thorough and unbiased as possible.
- Failure happens. Mark your wins. Don't let one wrong read overthrow all your correct ones.
- Other people will either believe you or they won't. Don't waste your time in fruitless debates.
- As long as all of your checks are in place, you are the only one who needs to believe you.
- There are other paranormal mediums and enthusiasts out there. You just need to find your people.

GLOSSARY

BASE POINT:

Your starting point with psychic perception (a kind of base camp for yourself). To find your base point, you have to first understand yourself, without looking outward either physically or psychically. Finding your base point is about understanding yourself.

CLAIRAUDIENCE:

One of the seven psychic senses, it is the ability to hear spiritual activity such as voices, music, sounds of the past, and so on. There are two main types: physical-ear clairaudience and inner-ear clairaudience.

CLAIRCOGNIZANCE:

One of the seven psychic senses, it is the ability to know new information that you could not have concluded in a straightforward manner based on your surroundings and personal knowledge. In essence, claircognizance is your intuition.

CLAIREMOTION/CLAIRSENTIENCE:

One of the seven psychic senses, it is the ability to feel a spirit's emotion, either through experiencing it within yourself or through knowing what emotion is in a room.

CLAIRGUSTANCE:

The most uncommon of the seven psychic senses, it is psychic taste.

CLAIRSALIENCE:

One of the seven psychic senses, it is the ability to smell something that is not physically there.

CLAIRTANGENCY/PSYCHOMETRY:

One of the seven psychic senses, clairtangency entails physically feeling sensations that cannot be detected or explained by the ordinary senses (for example, you may feel a chill or the touch of a hand on your own).

CLAIRVOYANCE:

One of the seven psychic senses, it is the ability to *see* spiritual or psychic information. There are two types: physical-eye clairvoyance and inner-eye clairvoyance.

CLEANSE:

To cleanse your energy is to wipe all external thoughts, feelings, emotions, sensations, and memories from your energy.

DEITY:

A spiritual being considered to be sacred or worthy of worship, often called a god or goddess. Deities are far from ghosts in terms of frequency, so often have very little to do with them.

DENSITY:

A material's density is the amount of mass it has per unit of volume. Humans and ghosts tend to have a heavy density, whereas passed loved ones and spirit guides have a higher density. High or low density does not equal good or bad.

DOWSING RODS:

A common psychic tool for validating ghost reads. They are a pair of *L*-shaped rods that you hold on to by grasping the shorter sides. The rods will cross like an *X* for a yes and move away from each other for a no. *Maybe* is the interpretation when one rod moves out and the other remains straight.

ELECTROMAGNETIC FIELD (EMF) METER:

A technology tool for validating your ghost readings. EMF meters are used to check for safe levels of electromagnetic waves in buildings and can also be used to detect spiritual activity. The more excited a ghost is about a subject, the higher the lights on the meter will flash.

FLAME/SMOKE:

A psychic tool used for scrying—that is, seeing and interpreting images in everyday things. Ghosts and other spiritual beings can sometimes make the flame of a candle burn tall and straight for yes or low and dull for no. Sometimes they can manipulate the smoke to flow in a particular direction.

FREQUENCY:

The number of cycles or vibrations a wave (for example, a sound wave) completes within a set amount of time. Sound frequency can be measured in hertz, and spiritual vibration can be measured in this way too, using paranormal investigative equipment.

GHOSTS:

Pieces of souls that are not ready to move on to the next plane of existence. A ghost may represent only a moment in a life.

GROUNDING (ENERGY):

Grounding your energy is how you stay connected to yourself no matter what spiritual or psychic information you may be getting. Mindfulness is the foundation for the grounding process and teaches you to start with yourself and your own energy before you journey into anything outside of yourself.

INHUMAN ENTITIES:

A type of spiritual entity. Sometimes they are a hybrid of various beings that can sit at different frequencies. Other inhuman beings can include anything from fae to aliens to mythological beasts.

INNER-EAR CLAIRAUDIENCE:

Feeling a spirit said something or *knowing* something was just said. This may feel like an inner dialogue with another in your head.

INNER-EYE CLAIRVOYANCE:

The more common type of clairvoyance, this is the ability to utilize the images of the mind's eye rather than the perceptions of the physical eye alone. Visions may come through as far- or nearsighted, and you can use your mind to focus in or zoom out accordingly to create the clearest possible picture.

INTUITION:

The ability to understand something without the need for reasoning. Often described as your gut feeling.

MEDIUM (PSYCHIC MEDIUM):

Someone who can act as a mediator between the spirit world and the physical world.

MINDFULNESS:

A mental state achieved by focusing on the present moment. Mindfulness allows you to observe your thoughts or feelings without judging them and achieve a sense of calm.

NON-SENTIENT ENERGY:

Also called *thought-form spirits*, this type of spirit is created by the energy of cognition. Examples may be visions of things long gone, sounds of guns on a battlefield, or phantom pains.

ORACLE CARDS:

A psychic tool for validating your reads and discovering the emotions and feelings of ghosts. When using oracle cards, you can look at the image provided on the card, allow your eye to be drawn to an aspect of that image, and utilize what it's trying to tell you from there. Some people like to ask for yes and no responses based on even- and odd-numbered cards.

PASSED LOVED ONE:

A catch-all term for anyone who has lived an incarnation and has since transitioned from our physical plane to the next. When this book refers to a *passed loved one*, it is referring to the fuller part of the once-incarnate soul—the part that does not get stuck behind.

PENDULUM:

A psychic tool used for validating readings, it is often a simple, light weight at the end of a chain or string. Some people ask the pendulum to move in a circle for yes and back and forth for no, while others may like to have their pendulum move clockwise for yes and counterclockwise for no. And still other people like to use a pendulum board with *yes*, *no*, *maybe*, and other words written out.

PHASMABOX:

An audio-based application that allows the individual using it to more easily hear the spoken words of spirits. It is produced by eXtremeSenses and is downloadable only for Windows computers.

PHYSICAL-EAR CLAIRAUDIENCE:

Hearing spiritual activity (voices, music, and so on) with your physical ears as opposed to *feeling* or *knowing* a sound.

PHYSICAL-EYE CLAIRVOYANCE:

The ability to see spiritual energy with your eyes. This may include, but is not limited to, seeing shadow figures, balls of light or orbs, figures with details, waves of energy, auras, and so on.

PSYCHIC:

A broad term referring to a person who knows information without having a physical source of the knowledge, meaning they didn't use standard senses to achieve the knowledge.

PSYCHIC BIAS:

The way in which you understand the world, often grown from the beliefs you have about the world or personal fears. Your psychic bias affects the way you understand your spiritual experiences.

PSYCHIC SENSES:

Your spiritual senses of perception. While these senses are often rolled into one idea called the *sixth sense*, there are seven individual psychics senses: Claircognizance, Clairvoyance, Clairaudience, Clairtangency, Clairemotion/Clairsentience, Clairsalience, and Clairgustance.

SHIELD:

Any way you protect your state of energetic balance. It is a spiritual manifestation of the mental protections and boundaries you keep for yourself.

SPIRIT GUIDES:

Entities who work specifically with you to help you on your life path. They can be your ancestors; someone who knew you from past lives or incarnations; your passed loved ones (even pets); or inhuman entities such as fae, elementals, and aliens.

SPIRITUAL PRACTITIONER:

Someone who is not only a psychic medium but can also reach into the spiritual plane and have an effect. For example, someone who is able to remove a spirit from a particular location.

THETA STATE:

A naturally occurring pattern of brain waves where the brain relaxes into a daydreamy or half-awake, half-asleep state. This is the state where the brain is most able to meditate to receive intuitive information for spiritual connection.

VIBRATION:

The inherent energetic quality of an object, environment, or person. Spiritual beings put out vibrations, just as those in the physical world naturally vibrate on a molecular level. Similar to electromagnetic vibration, much of the spectrum of spiritual vibration cannot be seen. But like vibrations in the physical world, spiritual vibrations can be felt, heard, and perceived, especially as they become more abundant.

ABOUT THE AUTHOR

Rebekah "The Ghost Guide" Carmichael is a polytheistic Quaker who is a proud advocate for teaching history, supporting small businesses, preserving the environment, speaking up for human rights, living a minimalistic lifestyle, van life, and saving animals from cruelty. While she enjoys being able to hop into her converted van and go anywhere her intuition leads her, she primarily splits her time between Wilmington, North Carolina, and Savannah, Georgia, with her beloved partner in all things life and death, Tharyn. Together they share a spooky little found family of ghosts, guides, and guardians.

For more information on how to work with Rebekah; her exclusive community, Twilight Lantern; and to meet her in group settings and one-on-one, please visit RebekahTheGhostGuide.com.

INDEX

D

H

I